94TH & RACINE

94TH & RACINE

The Roots of Me

BY

NYA B

iUniverse, Inc.
Bloomington

94TH & RACINE
The Roots of Me

iUniverse books may be ordered through booksellers or by contacting:

iUniverse
1663 Liberty Drive
Bloomington, IN 47403
www.iuniverse.com
1-800-Authors (1-800-288-4677)

ISBN: 978-1-4697-9443-3 (sc)
ISBN: 978-1-4697-9444-0 (hc)
ISBN: 978-1-4697-9445-7 (ebk)

Printed in the United States of America

iUniverse rev. date: 03/20/2012

DEDICATIONS

FOR THOSE WHO FLEW WITHOUT wings, loved without a heart and dreamed without ever sleeping . . .

For my boys . . . You may never see the life I lived but I want you to know that you come from strength, determination and perseverance. Please don't ever live your life without those 3 things.

CONTENTS

INTRODUCTION

(To protect the identities of friends and family,
most names and places have been changed)

I WAS BROUGHT IN THIS world unlike the traditions, unlike the plan but most certainly made to survive. Five pounds, three ounces and enough yellow jaundice to know that my mom was stressed. She told me she smoked cigarettes throughout the pregnancy just to calm her nerves and cope with her and my dad's unhealthy relationship. She said she loved him. It was almost as if he was her only chance at love. She believed in him and needed him like the air she breathed. Nevertheless, she thought he was the one and would've done anything for him. While I don't remember everything about their love, I do know that it seemed tainted. They were never married, once in love I suppose but from the stories I've heard, there were other people, lies, likes, dislikes, make up to break up and a lot of vengeance. While my parents didn't see eye to eye on monogamy, they agreed on one thing . . . ME.

I was born Cori B., April 3, 1981. I remember my mom sharing stories of that day as if it were yesterday. I was due on May 26th, her water broke weeks earlier and her step dad Ernest took her to the hospital, Roseland Community Hospital to be exact. While the details of the labor sound usual, there was one thing I remember most in my mom's story . . . my dad's absence. Now to some unwed mothers, the dad's absence may seem unfortunately typical.

However, when that mom has to get in touch with dad's current girlfriend to tell him that he has a daughter, the experience almost seems traumatic. I assume he got the message for he made it just in time to sign the birth certificate and give me that hideous name. According to my mom, my dad insisted on naming me Cori. While my mom had other plans for my name, she allowed it. I remember my mom telling me how hurt she was that soon after I was born, my dad married his girlfriend. She said he gave her a story about needing to be financially stable and with this other woman that became possible.

Like many couples who have children together, they continued to see one another. Financially broke or not, it seems they just couldn't get enough of each other or the drama. What drama do you ask? Oh, my mother was dramatic, some would say borderline crazy but she could definitely put on a show. She also knew how to get even. Summer 1983, she took my dad to a steppers club, the CopperBox, I recall. She said she had this plan to flirt and dance with other men as he watched. Needless to say it really upset my dad but in my mom's mind, that meant he cared. By winter 1985, she said she had enough of the infidelities and no tears could make my dad see how hurt she really was. Though Patsi was her name, get back was her game. The rise and fall of their relationship was just the beginning of who my mom really became . . . a woman scorned.

Chapter 1

Family

T HE ROOT TO EVERY HUMAN being begins with their family. I came from a large family and dysfunctional or not, they were a part of me and whether I wanted to admit it or not I was a part of them. I take from my family their ability to survive, their courage and most of all their deep seeded beauty.

My great grandmother Mae was one of nine children, one brother and eight sisters. Born and raised in Birmingham, Al, Mae was a beauty. She had big brown eyes, perfectly round face and skin as flawless as the moon. Her hair was flowing and oh so thick with a shine that reflected. Her style of dress was very chic. Although she could tell you where to go and how to get there, she had a heart that could warm an empty room. She was a seamstress, a musician and specialized in cosmetology. She cared about her appearance and cared very deeply about her daughter . . . my grandmother Reese. Now Reese was an only child. She was just as beautiful as her mother Mae. She had caramel shaded skin, at least 5'7 in height and just like Mae, could stop traffic with her beauty. When Reese was born, Mae headed north to find work. I heard that adjusting in a new town with a new baby in the 1930's was difficult so Mae left Reese behind. It wasn't too long after Reese's teenage years that she and Mae grace the streets of Chicago's south side. While I was too young to know the dynamics of Mae and Reese's relationship, I remember Mae and who she was to me. Once Mae moved to Chicago, she became a part of the nation of Islam. I remember her spending a lot of time with my older brother reading The Koran. When I would visit, she'd ask about my well being and it wasn't long before she'd try to convert me too. One time I had to stop her and say, "Hey Mae, I'm only six", she laughed. Nevertheless, she wanted our souls to be saved and Allah was the savior to do it. While we all had a positive relationship with Mae, Reese sometimes seemed to be easily aggravated with her. Reese had a strong faith in God and Jesus was her savior. We were all told to love Jesus too but Reese and Mae took religion rivalry to another level, so much so that it seemed to cause problems in their relationship.

Reese had her own problems, a house full of her own to raise and a marriage to save. My grandmother was a very strong and assertive woman. She was a survivor and managed to always say what was on her mind regardless of how others felt about it. The one thing that confused me the most about Grandma Reese was her struggle with religion. Although she was a Christian, a seriously saved woman, she could curse you out like you meant nothing to her then turn around and pray about it. She was also the best at quoting the Bible with a drink in her hand. I remember one time I talked back to her, she asked me to go outside and get a switch. As if getting my own switch wasn't enough, she had the nerve to tell me right before she whooped me that the Bible says spare the rod and ruin the child. I thought, "What?" I couldn't tell if she was a sinner or a saint and I guess that's why we *all* needed God's protection. I will never forget the time Reese pulled me from Lake Michigan. As we did most summers, we hung out downtown and sat on the rocks surrounding the lake. I imagine I played too close because I slipped off one of the rocks and fell in. I can remember going up and down in the water, trying really hard to catch my breath. I could hear Reese screaming above the water, "Grab my hand B, grab my hand." I kept my arm above the water so she could see it and sure enough, she grabbed me and pulled me up. The car ride home was a wet one but I was happy to be alive and it was Grandma Reese who saved me.

Reese worked hard and played hard. Because of her beauty and model like physique, keeping the men away was unheard of. When I think of Reese I can hear that song playing in my head, "poppa was a rolling stone" accept it was more like "grandma was a rolling stone". She was the mother of seven children. Her first two and born to different men, were my mom, Patsi and Aunt Cara. She later married the man we all knew as granddad and allegedly gave him five more, Darryl, Phyllis, Malcolm, Anthony, and Keith. Unfortunately, Darryl and Keith passed before I ever got a chance to know them but I heard that Phyllis and Darryl spent a lot of time with me, as in often mistaken for my parents. Speaking of parents, a very important dynamic about my family is that parents seldom raised their own children. They may have spent money, gave orders and made legal decisions but beyond that, the time spent was either with Grandma Reese or an aunt and uncle. They were my family and I was happy to belong, no matter what drama came our way.

It is my theory that *all* children are products of their environment. To understand me is to know Patsi, to understand my mother is to know Reese and so the story goes on. I was born and raised on the south side of Chicago, 94th and Racine. I was the middle child on both sides of my parent's family. I was raised with my mom's family so every moment with them sticks out like a sore thumb. With Patsi, I had two siblings, Darren and Brittany. Darren and I were very close. We were eight years apart yet in sync enough to be twins. He was my protector and couldn't stand for me to suck my thumb. Outside of soaking my thumb with hot sauce, I will never forget the day he played the meanest trick on me. It was fall of 1987; we attended a Catholic school, located on the southeast side. Each morning we would catch the "L" from 95th to 79th and take the 79th street bus going east. Darren walked really fast sometimes and I would always run behind, whining because I couldn't catch up. One morning it was time to get off the "L" and I must have been looking out the window too long because I looked over only to find he was no longer sitting beside me. I became hysterical. I jumped off the train before the doors closed and stood in the middle of the platform with my arms open as if God himself was coming to get me. Darren came running over to me laughing profusely, "Shut up girl, no one's going to leave you", he said. He grabbed me by my hand and off to school we went. Like many older siblings, tormenting me seemed to give Darren great pleasure. While he enjoyed turning me upside down as if change would fall from my pockets, he also enjoyed helping me learn. Our after school time was the best. Grandma Reese would fix us something to eat as Darren would help me with my homework. I remember him teaching me to sound out words and how to write my name correctly. He nicknamed me "the brain" for he believed I was smart and caught on quickly. In fact, I was so smart that I began to notice our homework time getting shorter and shorter.

While things were great between me and Darren, I remember our mom being frustrated with his actions. According to anyone who knew Darren, he was the type of teenager that made you cry and laugh at the same time. My mom described his behavior as sneaky and soon her patience ran thin. He stole for what he wanted but could hustle for what he needed. One summer evening of 1987, I walked into the living room of Grandma Reese's house. The living room was decorated with flowers, pictures, a wooden floor size television, a love seat along one wall and a chair along the other. The full size sofa sat in front of the window and in front of that, the coffee table. My mom had just awaken to find her car missing. She was sitting on the full size sofa just gazing out of the window. She was apparently angry because she kept repeating "that little muthafucka". It wasn't long before I realized that it was my brother she was speaking of. She believed he had stolen her car and boy did she have a plan for his punishment. She decided to stand in the bushes and surprise him when he returned home. The bushes stood thick in the front of the house making it difficult for anyone to notice someone standing in them. My brother pulled up and attempted to put the car back the way he found it. To his surprise the spot in which the car was initially parked was taken. It didn't matter anyway because mom had already figured him out. After he found another spot across the street, he got out of the car and began to walk towards the house. Mom jumped out from the bushes, terrifying my brother into an early grave. She then proceeded to do serious physical harm. I think this was probably the most memorable beat down I ever saw. My brother didn't fight back, he seemed to be in shock. I cried for him because I thought she was going to kill him. However, he survived and my mom later sent him to live with his father. I begged for him to stay just as he begged for my mom's forgiveness. It appeared to be too late. Patsi had enough and admitted that she could no longer raise a boy by herself. Darren continued to come to 94th and visit us. It seemed his dad was very strict with his curfew so I didn't see him as much as I used to. He continued to beg my mom if he could come home but she continued to refuse. In the fall of 1988, he began high school at an all-boys Catholic school. He seemed to be being doing well with his studies. I often overheard my mom bragging about his picture being in the Who's Who of High School Students. I never knew what Who's Who was or even the significance of the honor. I just knew I was happy that my brother was still in my life.

While my brother was very important to me, my entire family helped shaped the person I am today. The dynamics of my family was very interesting. If we had nothing at all, we definitely had each other. My family was not one of those families where you didn't know everyone in it. From Wisconsin to Alabama to Arizona, we all knew each other. My family was close and unfortunately I don't believe we realized how strong that really made us. We often fought and had tons of dysfunction but if one went down, we all did. What I admired most about my family was our ability to turn nothing into something. We celebrated every holiday and couldn't wait for the next reason to throw a party. Drugs, alcohol and jealousy would soon tear us apart but before I take you down that road, I must allow you to get to know everyone.

Many adults tend to be innocent through a child's eyes but there was one family member who I just could not stand . . . my aunt Cara. She was the meanest person I had ever met. When I first learned of her personality, I would forever know the definition of selfish. Like all the women in my family, Cara was very beautiful. She was tall and slender with the most flawless milk chocolate skin. She definitely could've been a model accept once she opened her mouth, she immediately became the ugliest person in the world. She always reminded me of Whitney Houston but I'm certain Whitney would've been a better aunt. None of us was ever allowed in Cara's room. She was like a vampire. The sun seemed to bother her so she slept all day and if you wanted her out of your face, present her with the holy cross and some garlic. I remember one Saturday morning Cara got up to make breakfast. My younger sister and I, Brittany were awaken by the smell of bacon and biscuits. We darted to the kitchen. As we stood there beside the stove, watching Cara flip one piece of bacon after the next, she looks down at us and asks, "What yall want"? "We're hungry", Brittany and I whined. "Well go find your momma; this is for me and Travis" she replied. Travis was my first cousin, Cara's only son at the time. He was two years older than me and six years older than Brittany. I think my mom must have overheard her because in she walks with messy hair and morning breath that lingered once she was no longer there. "You can't make my kids no food?" she yelled. "I just made enough for me and Travis! It's enough in there for you to cook your kids something to eat, damn", Cara shouted back. I don't recall my mom liking that answer because she began to call Cara every selfish bitch in the book. Brittany and I ran into the other room with Grandma Reese. "What is all this name calling about?" Grandma Reese asked as she walked towards the kitchen. "Your ugly ass daughter is selfish. She can let my kids starve but can fix her and her son something to eat," my mom shouted. "Ok, ok, Patsi, just calm down, it's more food in there. I just went to the grocery store so how about I fix the girls something." Meanwhile, Cara tells my mom to shut up and go back to bed. Grandma Reese stepped in and suggested that they both go back to bed and she will just cook for everybody. Brittany and I stood in the corner. Our cousin Travis was awakened by the yelling so he walked up and stood beside us. Like children did, we stood around quietly, trying to make sense of what just happened. I will never forget the way Cara exited the kitchen. She handed Travis his bacon and as she walked passed us, she took a slow bite of her bacon as if it were the last piece and she was the only one to get it. The look on her face as she stared at us said, "You're hungry aren't you"? My mom noticed it and shouted, "It may be early in the morning but I will kick yo' ass if you keep mistreating my babies." Cara shouted back, "Patsi, please!" and she closed her bedroom door. I don't remember seeing her again for the rest of the day. Nevertheless, Cara's selfishness set the tone for how I felt about her and would define our relationship for decades to come.

No one else in my family seemed to be as mean as Cara. While she was not my favorite, she was family and I had to respect her. However, I definitely had my favorites. I define my favorites as the ones I could go to no matter what. They understood that life happened. We spoke the same language and they accepted me for the little troubled girl I was. As I can say there were quite a few people I felt this way about. The person that stands out in my mind the most is my aunt Phyllis. She was the youngest girl of Grandma

Reese's children. She didn't look like the rest of us, meaning darker skinned. Her skin was extremely light. She was tall like everyone else just not as tall as Cara. She too was beautiful but that goes without saying. She loved to smile and I had an attachment to her that was unbreakable. She traveled a lot and always seemed to be having fun no matter what she was doing. I remember Phyllis and her girlfriends were getting ready to go see Janet Jackson. They sat in the kitchen one night just smiling at the cover of her new album, Control. I watched her get ready as she put on her makeup. First was the foundation, then the eyeliner, followed by the eye shadow and last, the lip stick which was then covered with a shine of lip gloss. As they all headed out, she and her friends checked themselves for flaws and I remember asking Phyllis as I pointed to one of her friends, "Is that Janet Jackson?" They laughed at me and one of her friends said "I wish." I asked if I could go and she politely told me, "No". Phyllis gave me a hug and a kiss and told me she would bring me back a poster. I remember going to sleep that night thinking, "I'm going to be just like her . . ." Phyllis was always sweet to me. When she spoke to me or called my name it was as if she was checking to see if I were ok. When she looked at me, it wasn't just a look, it was her saying to me "My baby niece, I'm here to save you."

While we all have family members that make us angry or make us happy, let's not forget the ones that makes us want to dance. When it came to parties and get-togethers, my uncles were the ones to hang with. They were loud, always excited but sometimes violent. My favorite uncle was Anthony. He was such a cutie and had the biggest glasses. The ladies seemed to love him and to this day I can't picture him single. Just like Phyllis, he was a sweetheart. While he sometimes didn't catch on as quick and seemed to let the ladies run over him, he was a joy to be around. He loved music and loved to DJ. I liked to call him "DJ one crate" because he always had that *one* crate of records. I remember hearing him in the attic on the turn tables and those words "Jack your body, jack, jack, jack your body." The base was sometimes annoying, especially for Grandma Reese. She would open that attic door and scream "Turn that shit down, Anthony!" The Bears, The Bulls and seeing the women shake their asses on Soul

Train were all reasons for Anthony to smile. I hated to see him hurt and my uncle Malcolm was usually the reason for that.

My uncle Malcolm could be nice but he sometimes scared me. He always thought I needed to be a man for some reason. He played rough with me all the time and always felt the need to teach me self defense. I have tons of memories with Malcolm but the one that stands out the most is when he hit me with an iron. It was one of those days I was getting a lesson in self defense. Like he usually did, he was walking around the house with no shirt on. I assume he was getting ready to iron one because he had the iron in his hand. Out of nowhere he says "B, come hit me as hard as you can. I wanna see if you can fight." I was only 8 at the time, so hey I did it. He flexed his chest muscles as if he were ready so I made a fist and punched him as hard I could, right in the chest. I don't think he expected me to hit him as hard as I did because his natural reflexes caused him to hit me with the iron in my forehead. I began crying so loud, he grabbed me and gave me a big hug, "Shhh, don't cry B, I'm sorry. You shouldn't have hit me so hard", he said. My head hurt for at least a week. Nevertheless, I loved Malcolm the same and while our relationship was bittersweet, I knew he would always have my back if I needed him to.

I don't have many memories of my other two uncles. As a matter of fact I don't have any at all. As I stated earlier, I never got to know Daryl. He died when I was only two years old, carbon monoxide poisoning, I was told. I heard stories about how one day Grandma Reese came home and found him and a lady friend smoking weed in the attic. Grandma Reese asked them to leave. Apparently they didn't finish their "joint" so they completed their smoke session in his car which was parked in the garage. I heard they cut the car on for heat since it was the middle of one of Chicago's coldest winters. I'm not certain what his thought process was but they failed to open the garage door to release the fumes. My mom said she went outside to check on Daryl after having a bad gut instinct. She said she cried and screamed as she found him and his lady friend dead. She told me that my uncle Malcolm helped her pull his body out of the car and laid him down on the ground. I can imagine that being very traumatic for her and I can also imagine how hard it was on Grandma Reese. Everyone shared stories with me about how Daryl loved having me with him when I was a baby. He took me everywhere with him whether I was dressed appropriate or not. I was told my other uncle Keith died as a toddler. There isn't much I can say about Keith accept it was reported that his cause of death was pneumonia.

While the adults in my family made 94th & Racine manageable, it was my siblings and cousins that made it feel like home. We got in trouble together, took baths together, slept in the same beds together and most importantly, witnessed all the drama and heartache together. Travis was my favorite cousin. He was also my first cousin. He was tall, skinny and very funny. He liked to laugh and sometimes did a horrible job at being the oldest. People always mistook me and Travis for brother and sister and to think about it, we kind of were. I could go on for days with the memories. However, what I remember most about Travis are our arguments. Grandma Reese would sometimes let us have one dollar from the food stamp book; the brown one. She sent me and Travis to the store, Mr. G's to be for certain. Travis somehow convinced me that since he was older, he was supposed to get the dollar. With that dollar, he bought himself a bag of candy and some Reese's Peanut Butter Cups. If he didn't share with me, I found myself destroying whatever it was he had. I asked him if I could have a piece of his peanut butter cup and he told me "No." I quietly accepted his answer but as he lifted his hand to put the last cup in his mouth, I squeezed his hand with the peanut butter cup in it with the hopes of turning it to mush. Immediately that anger I had turned to happiness and Travis was furious. If I couldn't have a peanut butter cup, neither could he.

Just as Travis hated sharing with me, I hated sharing with Brittany. Brittany was my little sister and four years younger than me. She was also a twitch in my left eye. She was so cute. Much of the family believed we didn't get along because I was jealous of her. She was of course lighter than I was. She had the cutest round cheeks and because she sucked her thumb, she had an overbite. I must say that jealousy was not the issue. She in fact irritated me. Brittany did almost anything she could to upset me. She seemed to spend a lot of her time stealing my panties because hers weren't clean or trying to wear my shoes knowing she couldn't fit them. She lied as if it were a first language and played the victim like she could do no wrong. However, regardless of what she did, I couldn't stop loving her. She often gave her last to people whether they deserved it or not. Because she was my baby sister, I had to protect her and show her the importance of respecting other people's property. Little did I know, getting close to her would be a struggle.

When my uncle Daryl died, he left behind two children, my cousins Zee and Donte. Zee was raised by her family who stayed right across the alley and like Reese did with the rest of her grandchildren, she raised Donte. Donte was the silent type. He was sweet and would do anything for me. He was the chubby cousin. I'm ashamed to say Travis and I always teased him about his weight, breathing habits and the fact that it took him forever to be potty trained. While it may have been mean, it was definitely funny. His nickname was "pee-pee boy." I hated sharing a bed with Donte. I remember one night, aunt Cara didn't come home (Thank God) and Grandma Reese made me and Donte sleep in her bed. I begged Grandma Reese to let me sleep with her but Brittany had already taken the spot. While Donte never really got on my nerves or did anything to me, I just couldn't sleep with him. I didn't want to sleep on the floor and let the roaches get me so I felt compelled to give it a shot. Grandma Reese made Donte go to the bathroom before bed but that didn't help. I woke up the next morning covered in piss as if I had slept in the toilet. It was at that moment, I believed that sleeping with the roaches may not have been such a bad idea.

Being with my family can be very fun. We had parties, celebrations for absolutely no reason at all, barbeques at the nearest Forest Preserve and holidays that will never be forgotten. Summers in Chicago were very exciting. We hung out at the Taste, watched fireworks, played at Great America and took advantage of the outside. Christmas was always the best as a child. Grandma Reese always did what she could. I remember one Christmas, Brittany and I got our first real Barbies; not the ones from the dollar store that were barely made of plastic but the ones we saw on the commercials. We were so excited and couldn't wait to tell our friends that we got *real* Barbies. To have a real Barbie meant you were something special and your family had status. I think many people knew that we didn't have money but what made us popular was our ability to treat everyone like family. I would never describe my family as "funny acting." They were the most "down to earth" people anyone could meet. While boundary setting and tact may have been a problem, feeling at home with them was not.

One of the things that made my family whole was the nonstop list of cousins. I didn't have cousins that I didn't know or dealt with from a distance. Mae and Grandma Reese made sure we knew everyone from Birmingham to Wisconsin to the southeast side of Chicago. Growing up, I can honestly say all my cousins were important. Outside of the ones I lived with, my cousins in Wisconsin were just as influential. While I enjoyed visiting Wisconsin for the summer, I would just die with boredom and beg to go home early. My cousin Livee was serious about having one us from 94th spend part of the summer with her. Somehow I was always the chosen one. I will never forget the summer I sang at her church. During Livee's choir rehearsal, she mentioned I could sing. The pianist asked me to sing a song and I imagine they wanted it to be gospel but the only song that came to mind was, "The Greatest Love of All" by Whitney Houston. When it came to a crowd, I never felt shy. To stand in front of a crowd always seemed to be very energizing and motivating. The most fun I had that summer included a swimming accident in which I almost drowned *again* and us getting into a car accident on the way to Chicago. Traumatic one would think, but nonetheless, the highlight of a trip to Livee's.

While I enjoyed connecting with Livee, I always enjoyed the relationships with the cousins I could relate to. When it came to my cousins, Keena, Connie and Lori, I knew it was with them that I would have the most fun. Keena and Connie were the closest to my age. They were in-laws but one couldn't tell by our connection. Summers with Keena and Connie were always interesting. I loved having them around and we spent a lot of time comparing. I think it's natural for young ladies to compare themselves to those they are closest to. There was something about each of them I greatly admired. Keena was very pretty. She had the deepest dimples and the prettiest skin. She was more developed than I was and every time I saw her, I would say to myself "When will I get my breasts?" Connie on the other hand was more like me when it came to our body types but she was light skinned. It seemed everywhere we went, the boys wanted *her*. She had the most beautiful hair, the prettiest hands and feet, flawless skin and goofiness out of this world. We were a lot closer than Keisha and I were and at some point, I may have considered her a best friend. Connie and I shared secrets, clothes, laughter and as we got older, boyfriends. Our relationship would later fade just as smoke did but it never changed who she was to me. Unlike Keena and Connie, Lori was much older than I was, 9 years older to be exact. Like most of my extended family members, Lori was light-skinned. She was short in height and had the beauty of a goddess. Lori had sandy brown hair, high cheek bones, eyes in the shape of almonds and a sweet personality to match. On the outside looking in, Lori had a life to die for. She had boyfriends from college and one could tell she was very popular because she was always on the go. If there was anyone in my family qualified to give me a "hand-me-down," it was Lori. I didn't mind getting the things she had because it was the only time I received something name brand. She lived with her grandmother, my great Aunt, Bessie. I enjoyed going over to her house just to play in her room. She had the bed of a princess. Her room was draped in pink with pink curtains, a pink bed spread and a pink canopy. She had dolls; Black dolls, a radio, board games and pictures all on the wall. I was proud to say she was my cousin and couldn't wait for the day we could hang together.

The list of cousins goes on and on and each of them has impacted my life in one way or another. Things were great on 94th as long as there was a party. Sometimes too much partying and not enough responsibility can make a household very unproductive. Sooner or later, somebody's going to struggle with the bills, children will begin to witness too much and heartache and pain takes over. Tragedy would soon tear my family apart and who people really were became very clear to me.

Chapter 2

Lost Love

I T HAD ALMOST BEEN A year since my brother lived with us. He continued to visit and rumor had it that he was being physically abused by his dad. I also heard rumors that he was becoming interested in being a "Stone". I was too young to know what being a "Stone" meant but nevertheless it was a gang. My brother often spent nights out on the street because he didn't want to go to the dungeon he called home. Patsi continued to refuse him coming to live with us. She was still convinced he needed a man to raise him. On February 20, 1989, Darren became ill. While he and his dad's family lived on the south side of Chicago, they traveled west to seek medical attention. The hospital sent him home with a diagnosis of the flu. February 21, 1989, Darren continued to be ill. It seems the "flu" just wasn't letting up. I imagined he pulled himself together good enough to take a shower, after awhile of being in there, he collapsed. It didn't seem like my brother was getting any better. I remember my mom being very worried and rightfully so, her only son, her first born was in the emergency room for reasons unknown. The entire family waited patiently and we all just knew Darren would be ok. I'm not sure Brittany knew what was going on but I certainly did. I sat up in Grandma Reese's living room on the love seat, farthest away from the window. I was wrapped in a blue blanket, eyes drooping from being so tired. After being gone for a few hours, my mom walked into the living room. I remember asking her if Darren was alright and she said in a very low tone, "He didn't make it." It was at that very moment, I felt a part of me die too.

I don't think I knew the effects of attachment until I lost my brother. For a while I asked myself the same questions, "Who's going to help me with school work? Who's going to play with me? Who's going to protect me?" I never got any answers and I guess I figured it out along the way. The funeral was unbearable. I wore a polka dot black and white dress with ruffles. My shoes were patent leather with white tights and ruffled socks. I stumbled as it was my turn to view his body. With a hand full of tears, I touched his face. The makeup smeared in one hand and in the other was a nickel. I leaned up and kissed him. Just like his face, his lips were cold. I began to get scared. This was the first time I consciously came in contact with a dead body. Nevertheless I was taking up too much time so I placed the nickel in his pocket and walked out of the church. I made it to the restroom and broke down, crying. I cried as if it was my life that ended and in many ways, I felt it had.

Of course I wasn't the only one who took Darren's death to heart. The entire family felt a void. He left behind a journal, awards, positive report cards and many joyful memories. While I never got use to living without him, I believe someone needed to be strong for my mom's sake. Patsi's pain was more than just the loss of a child. I think she carried a lot of guilt and anger. I think she was angry with Darren's dad and stepmom for what she believed to be careless attempts to seek medical attention. Patsi had a question for everything. In her mind, this entire situation could've been avoided. I can hear her now, "Why travel to the west side when there are great reputable hospitals here out south? Why diagnose with the flu when it was clearly pneumonia?" Then there was one question she would never say out loud, "Why didn't I let my son come home?" Patsi would never admit it but I know she felt guilty. The guilt began to show in almost everything she did. While the pain of losing my dad initiated her abuse of alcohol, losing my brother seemed to increase it.

The year was now 1990 and while I'm missing Darren every day, I'm slowly learning to live without him. To keep busy, Patsi worked full time and attended cosmetology school part-time. When she wasn't working, she was drunk and I began to have more responsibilities. While I still had my family, things didn't seem normal anymore. To mentally break away, I began to explore the other part of me . . . my dad. Charles was always a part of my life. He would come visit me every now and again just enough for me to remember who he was. Charles seemed to be very big on legacy and while he wasn't spending real time, he made sure I carried his name. My dad's favorite style of dress was a black leather vest with a black tank top. To add variety, he wore black jeans with black cowboy boots and a black hat. Oh and let's not forget the button he wore on his head that illustrated the red, black and green flag. To this day, I don't think I've seen him wear anything different. With legacy on the brain and an opportunity, I believe he thought it was time for me to get to know my other older brother. His name was Jackson. Jackson was six years older than I was and looked exactly like my dad. My dad had this obnoxious habit of introducing to me to people and saying "Cori, this is your cousin, now give 'em a hug." Needless to say I felt very awkward when I spent time with him. Charles was a lady's man and no matter how hard he tried to hide his lady friends, Jackson and I could always spot them a mile away.

One summer, my dad came to 94th to pick me up. As he did every time he parked his car, he got out and wiped it down. He drove a Cadillac, not sure of the type I just remember it being long and black. It must have taken him at least ten minutes before he actually began walking towards the door. Now that I was older, it seemed my mom was more compliant with letting me go with him. Later that day he took me and Jackson to a wedding. During the reception, this strange lady and her son kept talking to us. It wasn't just any conversation. It was one of those conversations where one could tell that she was phishing for information. Information that almost said, "Hey, this little boy next to me is your little brother and I've been seeing your daddy." Jackson and I shared the same puzzling look as we talked to her and it was at that very moment, I felt connected to him.

Jackson and I continued to keep in touch but because we shared different mothers, our getting together was minimal. Having my dad around was happy for me yet seemed hurtful for my mother. One could tell that she really wasn't dealing with their breakup in conjunction with the death of Darren very well. I never understood it but my parents seemed to have this peculiar relationship. When my dad wasn't around, Patsi would talk about him badly and when she'd see him, she would smile and laugh with him as if they were still in love. Although Patsi had physically moved on, I could tell that she was stuck. She always had a man and just like all the women in my family getting one of those was not difficult. Patsi was the first of her siblings and she set the tone for style better than any of them. I liked to call her Ms. Jazzy. In her younger years she wore the perfect afro. She had a figure eight shape and a smile that made the brothers weep. Her sweet scent lingered as she got ready for work, Exclamation was the smell. Patsi learned early how to play the game. She had no problem getting what she wanted and in her mind she had everything but love.

If anyone asked Patsi about love, she would be quick to tell them, "Don't nobody love me." A blind man could see that she had unresolved issues with Grandma Reese. I remember every morning, around 5am, Patsi and Grandma Reese would get up, sit at the kitchen table and gossip. Patsi had her cigarettes and Grandma Reese had her coffee. They talked about everything from men to lazy people in the house to who needed voodoo. It wasn't long before one of them said or did something the other one didn't like then the fighting began. I can remember at least two physical fights Grandma Reese and Patsi had. One fight ended with Grandma Reese hitting Patsi in the head with a flower vase. I'm not sure how the fight started. I just remember seeing my grandmother's hand tightly wrapped around my mom's throat. As my mom struggled to fight back, the vase broke right over her head. While I don't deny the idea that my mom probably said or did something to provoke it, no child should witness their parent in a fight. Grandma Reese and Patsi seemed toxic to one another. It was as if my mom wanted something from Grandma Reese that she just couldn't give and since it was missing, there was no way, she could give it to me.

Saturday, March 31, 1990. Patsi had this bright idea to give me and Brittany a shared birthday party. She said she didn't have money at the time to give Brittany a celebration and she didn't want Brittany to feel left out. Brittany's birthday is in February, a long way from April if you ask me but I assume Brittany needed her attention as well. Nevertheless, I had this domineering personality. I demanded attention and it was *my* birthday so there were no worries on how this day would turn out and besides, I don't recall even being looked at on Brittany's birthday. I was turning 9 and all my friends were going to be there. It was going to be a great party on 94th that day. Rita, Tee, Lucky and Megan were all my closest girlfriends. 1st grade class is where we met and they were the first invites on my list. The neighborhood kids were like my cousins, Peaches, Neicy, Mika and, Chyna and they too were all in attendance. I wore a white dress with sky blue ruffles along the bottom. Brittany wore a pink dress that flowed like Cinderella's and she had the cutest bow in the back. Patsi paid for a clown and we had the best food with party favors, candy, decorations and music. My gifts were excellent. I received one hundred dollars. It was the most money I ever had and I was excited to spend it. Unfortunately, Patsi said I owed it to her for the birthday party so she gladly gave me ten dollars and pocketed the rest. Immediately this party went from the best to the worst I ever had. I was extremely sad and while the other adults came to my defense it only made Patsi angrier. I can still hear her now, "I paid for his party, and this is my money." No one wanted to argue with Patsi because she was a force to be reckoned with. It was as if she believed the world owed her something. It felt like I owed her something.

When Patsi wasn't being unreasonable or letting the liquor speak for her, she was the most delicate woman. She was giving; she listened and was a completely different person. Like everyone else in the world, Patsi wanted love. She didn't seem to get it from Grandma Reese so she opted for the next best thing, a man. She wanted a husband to take care of her and her girls and she probably would've dealt with anything to have it. While my mom had several male friends including Brittany's dad, there was one that stuck around longer than any of them. His name was Carl. Carl was very handsome. He stood about 6 feet with hazel eyes and had a passion for my mom one wouldn't believe. I never knew what he did for employment. I just knew it was a great day when he came around. We always ate out and Connie's pizza was the place to go. Carl became the man Brittany and I knew as stepdad. Brittany loved Carl and hung on to his every word. He asked us to call him "Daddy Carl." I refused to call him "Daddy Carl" because he wasn't my daddy! While I enjoyed Connie's pizza, I really didn't like Carl. There was something about him that said trouble. He and I argued most of the time and it was mostly because he tried to tell me what to do. No matter how much he and I argued, there was no getting rid of Carl. He was Patsi's bread and butter and I or anyone else was going to mess that up for her.

Carl and Patsi had been together since I was five years old. I imagine he was there for her in a way that no other man had been. He was her provider, her caregiver, and the type of man she said she always wanted. Unfortunately like many women, she had no idea what to do with him once she had him. Patsi was very insecure when it came to Carl. She accused anyone with a vagina of wanting him, especially Grandma Reese. I remember when Patsi and Grandma Reese argued, my mom often told her that she was jealous of her because she had a man. According to Patsi, Grandma Reese was not only jealous of her having a man, she was even more bothered because that man was Carl. Grandma Reese would just laugh it off but it seemed the laughing got old and Grandma Reese had taken all the accusations she could take. As a result, Patsi was asked to leave 94th. Grandma Reese said there were too many grown women living under one roof. Since Patsi had this "delusion" about people always taking things from her, she took me and Brittany along with her. Patsi's coming and going on 94th was a pattern. Although she left many times before, she had always returned. This time around, she said she wasn't coming back and for a while, it seemed she meant it.

We relocated to 93rd and Laflin. It was a nice two bedroom apartment with friendly neighbors and more space. While Brittany and I still had to share a room, it was nice to have a place to call home. Although Carl didn't live with us, he visited very often. Sometimes Brittany and I were happy when he came and other times we couldn't wait to see him leave. I'm sure Patsi's mood had a lot to do that. If Patsi was happy, so were we and if she was miserable, we felt that too. Unfortunately, almost anything would trigger her sadness. It seemed there were things in life she just couldn't let go of and Carl for some reason reminded her of many things, especially my dad. Carl wasn't the most faithful man or at least Patsi didn't think so. If he didn't show up when he was supposed to or call at the allotted times, Patsi would get that "feeling." This feeling often told a woman whether or not her man was cheating.

May 1990, Patsi was in the living room listening to Aretha Franklin's, "Do Right Woman." She'd start off singing and then she'd get quiet. I could tell she was thinking about something because she never took her eyes off the floor. Her cigarette smoke arose in the air as she took small sips of her drink, gin and lime juice was always her choice. I could hear the ice cubes rattling in the glass. It wasn't long before she noticed Brittany and I watching her then she yelled at us to go to bed. We hated to see her sad and no matter how much she tried to hide it, we always knew. We weren't asleep very long before we were awakened by Patsi asking us to get dressed and take a ride with her. Sleepy and tired, Brittany and I put on our coats and shoes and jumped into the car. I took my spot in the front seat, eager to go back to sleep. Between V103 and the cigarette smoke, sleep was almost impossible. It must have been around 1 in the morning. I remember seeing the "L" to the left side of me and the numbers on the exit signs going down. We exited on 40 something street. I assume we arrived at our destination because Patsi began to slow down. She looked around as if she wanted to spot something or someone. I'm certain she spotted it because she angrily parked the car. We were in the parking lot of a high rise building. There weren't many people in sight. They were probably asleep with the rest of Chicago. Patsi got out of the car, "I'll be right back," she said. I turned to look at Brittany and she was asleep. I followed Patsi with my eyes as far as they would take me. It's like she disappeared into the night. She didn't seem to be gone very long. Out of nowhere she jumped back into the car. She lit another cigarette and drove off as if she had just robbed a bank. I looked at her while she ranted and raved, "That muthafucka think he slick, got some bitch over his house. I got something for his ass, huh." Whenever Patsi ended a statement with "huh," she had a plan and was destined to follow through with it.

Like many 9 year olds, I didn't know the fundamentals of relationships. I knew that when my mom was mad at Carl, it was only a matter of time before they were back together. They could pick up as if nothing ever happened. I never liked to see Patsi in pain. As I got older, I found myself taking on a lot of Patsi's battles when it came to Carl. While she seemed to get over things and move forward, my dislike for him became stronger. I don't think Brittany had a mean bone in her body, but I on the other hand could be mean and stayed that way as long as I needed to. I spent a lot of time ignoring Carl, disrespecting him, cursing at him and hanging up on his friends when they called. It may not have been the nicest thing to do but, boy did it feel great! It seemed that when Patsi was angry at Carl, my disrespect seemed appropriate and in fact she encouraged it. On the other hand when she needed money or attention, I was supposed to be nice and that became very confusing. I realized then that my personality was not that flexible and this was only the beginning of our mother/daughter bond gone sour.

I'm certain that my attitude towards Carl didn't encourage him to embrace me the way he did Brittany. They laughed and played together. He bought her candy and gifts and sometimes I was jealous. Other times, I convinced myself that I was too old for that type of attention. Somehow I needed to find my way and getting in the middle of my mom's relationship was not the route to take. We didn't stay on 93rd and Laflin long. I don't know why. I assume the lease was up or maybe Patsi didn't like the location but nevertheless, we moved again. This time we relocated to 84th & Paulina.

One would think that with all the moving, it would be difficult for me and Brittany to attain and maintain friends. Ironically, making friends and keeping them wasn't difficult at all. As a matter of fact, we visited 94th every day. The limited time spent there seemed to make the relationship between Patsi and Grandma Reese much better. When they weren't having their reunions at the kitchen table, they were on the phone. One could tell they missed each other, until the moments where Patsi brought up the past and Grandma Reese blew it off. Her trips to the liquor store weren't too far behind those moments and that was me and Brittany's cue to disappear.

Patsi's parenting skills were hit or miss. While she never neglected us physically, it seemed that emotionally she wasn't there. Brittany and I always looked nice. Patsi was a beautician in her own right so our hair was always done. We were clean. We had nice shoes, pressed jeans and most importantly, we had each other. We never considered ourselves to be poor for everyone around us seemed to be living similar lifestyles and if they weren't, I don't remember them making us feel like we were any less. The majority of our peers were on free and reduced lunch. Each of our peers had at least one drug addict in the family or emotionally unstable person. While a few household members on 94th worked steady jobs, only one of them had a high school diploma and that was Grandma Reese. Patsi blamed Grandma Reese all the time for why she didn't complete high school. According to Patsi, Grandma Reese's absenteeism at a high school function was the beginning of an education gone bad. Patsi attended high school in the 70's. I remember she use to share stories with me and Brittany about the "Mother's Tea". She still sounded excited as she told us the story. It was a social event that allowed mothers and daughters to meet, greet and mingle with one another. Patsi said she really wanted to go. Unfortunately Grandma Reese wasn't interested. According to Patsi, Grandma Reese was drunk and allegedly cursed her out for even asking. Patsi said she was so hurt that she didn't even bother going back to school. I assume she really wanted to hurt Grandma Reese but in the end, it seemed she only hurt herself. I know Patsi struggled financially. I remember her car being repossessed, us having to move; utilities were on one day and off the next. Nevertheless, she did the best she could without me and Brittany ever feeling less privileged.

Chapter 3

Self Identity

I T IS MY THEORY THAT before any individual can effectively connect with others, they must first learn who *they* are. Who we are and how we feel about ourselves is determined by family, socioeconomic status and strengths. Eric Erickson was a psychoanalyst who believed that in order for individuals to be successful in life, they must master the eight stages of psychosocial development. Erickson would say I mastered the first three stages very well. I learned to trust. I had a great sense of autonomy and I took initiative on most things. However, I was stuck at a stage that took me a while to surpass and that was self-identity.

While self identity is a stage Erickson says takes 6 years to develop, it seemed it took me longer. Between the ages of 10 and 18, I didn't like myself. I thought I was unattractive and lacked talent. Much of how I felt about myself came from my family, my peers and their obsession with lighter skin. While I had darker skinned family members, it seems we weren't praised or cared for as much as those with lighter skin. No one would probably admit it but there was an extreme difference between the fair skin, the light skin and the dark. When Brittany and I argued, Patsi would yell at me and say "You're just mad at her because she's prettier and lighter than you." At that time, all I could say was that it wasn't true. I later began to question, "Am I jealous? Do I wish I were light skinned?" I didn't know what to think so I began to believe that I *was* jealous. I refused to spend time with Brittany. I began to feel like she was the "special" one and I was the one they were stuck with. I will never forget asking Patsi about why I was so dark. She told me this story about how this lady walked up to her car window and gave me to her when I was a baby. Other family members went along with the story and it made me even more confused. Sometimes I would believe them and other times, I was skeptical. Nevertheless, no one came out and said they were just playing. While I didn't feel great about myself or my skin color, I knew I wasn't alone. My cousin Travis and Uncle Malcolm seemed to share the same experience.

My great grandmother Mae seemed to really despise my skin color. It wasn't just the difference between me and Brittany that heightened my insecurities. It was the way my family treated me.

When I would spend the night with Mae, bath time before bed was imperative. She would run the water, put some bleach in the water and tell me to get in. I asked her "Mae, why do I need bleach in the water, Brittany didn't need it." She replied "It's a sin for you to be this dark, B. God didn't intend for it to be that way." As a child, it's easy to think that adults are always right and so I believed her. I wanted to scrub the sin away as much as she did. Putting bleach in the bathwater became the thing to do for a while. Grandma Reese adopted the same beliefs and we had to scrub until there was some "black" in the tub. I don't think it ever occurred to anyone that maybe DNA was the reason for my skin color. According to them, it was a sin or a curse. One can imagine how I internalized all of that and so I behaved accordingly.

Not feeling very good about myself began to be very apparent in my behaviors. While I kept a smile on my face, I was angry most of the time. People described me as mean, selfish and snappy. I fought most of the time, thanks to my insecurities yet strong need for friendship. I attended elementary school up the street and for the sake of names, I'll refer to it as "Southside Boogie". As many children can be, the students there were cruel. My nickname was "Cori Dookie Brown" or "Spook-a-nanny." I found myself going to school angry so it didn't take much for me to curse at another child or hit one unprovoked. One would think that with *so much* attitude, I would have a difficult time making friends. Fortunately, I didn't. My closest friends at this time were Megan, Tee, Lucky, Rita and June. I loved those girls. When others made me feel bad, they made me feel better. Tee was just as dark as I was, maybe even darker and not once did I see her struggle with complexion the way I did and I believe that's how we became close. I can't recall the connection between me and the others. I think it was just a matter of loyalty. As loyal as 10 year olds can be, we were it. However, regardless of what type of friends I had at school, I still struggled with who I was and who I wanted to be.

I had my friends at school but it seemed that's where I was only aloud to see them. Megan stayed a block over from me but my family never wanted me to go there. Racine was where I was bound and for that reason, the girls on my block tended to have the most influence on me. One young lady in particular definitely had an effect on everybody. She seemed to be the reason drama went down and the reason it didn't. Her name was Peaches. Peaches probably wouldn't admit this then, but she was a bully. She brought the kids on the block together and she'd pull them apart. Nevertheless, we all hung out at her house and followed her every instruction. Many of the adults on the block didn't seem to like Peaches or her influence. I know for a fact none of the adults in my house did but there was something about her that made us kids want to be around her. Peach's was tall with milk chocolate skin, a nice grade of hair and a nice sense of style. One could tell that she was taken care of yet she had a demeanor that was very disrespectful and controlling. I imagine that Peaches was two or three years older than I was. She and Travis had the most peculiar relationship. One day they'd be the best of friends and the next they'd physically fight. One could tell that they cared about one another because it was difficult for them to stay away from each other. I imagine they had a real friendship, toxic and all. Every day during the summer, Travis and I would run down to Peaches' house to do something we didn't have any business doing. We'd ride our bikes to 87th street Forest Preserves, ride down the hill or stay at Peaches' and play "house." Every time we played "house," Peaches got married to Travis and I got married to her younger brother. I did whatever Peaches asked me to do and mainly because I feared what would happen if I didn't. Peaches was very intimidating. When things didn't go her way, she'd yell and scream and sometimes become violent. Some would ask, "B, why do you hang around her?" Well the answer to that was simple. Peaches had the cutest little brother ever and he was the first to ever make me feel like I mattered. Every time I would go to Peaches' house his face would light up and so would mine. For the first time as a child, I knew that when he looked at me, he didn't see "Blacky" or "patent leather," he saw B. We called him "Chubb" and why I have no clue because from where I stood, there was nothing chubby about him. He had the cutest smile, with the highest cheek bones, the smoothest skin and most importantly, he thought I was pretty. Chubb was my first kiss (with peanut butter and jelly on the breath), my first hug, my first date at his kitchen table and my first play husband. I became obsessed with his validation and being controlled by his sister was something I was willing to go through if it meant seeing him. Chubb and I's innocent courtship would soon be cut short by his mother. Rightfully so, we were children and someone needed to step in to remind us of that. One summer day, Peaches had just completed another wedding ceremony. We all decided to lay down in the living room and take a nap. Chubb was holding me as we lay on the floor and in comes his mom with a white leather strap. She tore Peaches and Travis up first before she got to me and Chubb. Needless to say I was terrified and for the first time had been whooped by someone else's mother. Chubb's mom got on the phone and called down to Grandma Reese, "Your granddaughter is down here courting," she yelled. I could hear Grandma Reese all the way down the street, "B, get your fast ass in this house." For some reason, my ass was never just an ass, it was a fast one. I walked very slowly that day because I knew that I would get another whooping as soon as I got home.

When you're a child, adults don't believe you have any problems. Unfortunately, I had many of them, just not the kind my family felt were important. I continued to hang with Peaches and continued to have my title as "fast." The neighborhood didn't like it, my family definitely didn't like it and I still wasn't sure if I liked it but I had a friend and that's all that mattered. There were tons of girls on my block and if Peaches felt we were getting too close without her, she made sure, the bonds didn't last long. Outside of me, Brittany and Peaches, the 94th street girls included E, G, Lucy, Nikki, Niecy, Mika and Chyna. E lived directly across the street from me on 94th and her Godparents very seldom let her come outside. However, she was just as important to me as all the others. She was younger than I was and I remember her Godmother always acknowledging how she and I looked alike. I imagine it was because we both were dark with high cheek bones and full lips. It was almost as if that was the reason we needed to get to know each other. About two houses down from E was G. G and I knew each other but were never really friends.

We hung out sometimes but not as much as I did with the others. Many people on the block made fun of G because of her weight but she never seemed to let it bother her. She was the child on the block that had everything. She had toys, a beautiful home, both parents and hair for days. I don't think Peaches liked her too much because she kept her distance and was probably one of the few she couldn't control. G had the most handsome brother. He was light skinned, an athlete and clearly into Lucy. Lucy lived two houses down from me. You wouldn't know it today but she was definitely someone I considered a friend. Her grandmother use to have the coolest things for us to do in the summer time like make art projects using dough and paint. I believe Peaches tried very hard to keep us apart and for the most part she made us fight a lot. I know you're wondering, how can someone make two people fight? On 94th, it didn't take much. I will never forget, the summer of 1991. Lucy and I had been getting along great. This particular day, the 94th girls were jumping rope in Peaches' driveway. Double-dutch can go wrong when there is someone on the end turning in a way that we liked to call "underhanded." Either I didn't want to be on the end or I was angry that I didn't get a turn. Either way, I was not happy with Peaches. Peaches had this thing where if she was upset with you, others had to be upset with you too. She somehow convinced Lucy to turn on me. There was an argument that led to Lucy punching me in the stomach. Oddly enough, Peaches instructed me to hit her back and so I did it. There we were, two friends fighting, while Peaches sat back and watched. It felt good to fight Lucy, although I didn't have a clue as to why. It was at that moment, I truly felt hate for myself.

There were only a handful of people on the block that Peaches did not intimidate and that was Nikky, Niecy, Mika and Chyna. Nikki stayed across the street from Peaches. She was a sweetheart. You could tell that Peaches was jealous of her. I remember people describing Nikki as stuck up or thinking she's "all that." I often reached out to Nikki because she was pretty and she could jump double-dutch better than any of us. Nikki's parents seemed really strict. She was always caring for her two little brothers and didn't get to come outside very often. That was probably a good thing considering the amount of drama there was. However, the drama would soon cease. Especially after Niecy, Mika and Chyna hit the block. Niecy, Mika and Chyna were sisters that lived on the corner of 94th. For the sake of naming each of them, I will call them "the sisters." Like many sisters should do, they stuck together. For whatever reason, they seemed to be the only people on the block that Peaches respected. When Darren was alive, he and Chyna (the oldest of the sisters) dated briefly and it appeared that because of that, she would always look out for me and Brittany. I remember Chyna being dark like me. She wore this asymmetric hair cut and had dimples deep enough to swim in. I was drawn to people who wore dark complexion with confidence, hoping some of it would rub off on me. I began trying to look like her. Whatever she wore, I wore. The only thing I couldn't wear were the biking shorts, you know the ones with the fluorescent strip down the side. They were very popular in the 90's and Chyna wore them faithfully. She had them in every style; black and white, black and hot pink, black and orange and black and green. I begged Patsi for a pair but she insisted I was too young to wear them. The sisters very seldom hung out on the block. However, when they did, they too would hang out with Peaches but soon began to distance themselves. I believe they grew tired of Peaches' manipulation and desire for control. It wasn't long before they took me under their wing and taught me how to defend myself against her or anybody else that wanted to control me. Mika was like my teacher. She taught me the most inappropriate punches and kicks a young girl could ever learn. She always told me that if someone was too big for me to fight, to come and get her. Mika was at least five years older than I was; Chyna was 7 years older and Niecy was maybe 3 or 4. Later that summer, Chyna gave birth to a baby girl so I didn't get to see her as much. I soon began spending all my time with Mika and Niecy. Grandma Reese didn't like me hanging with them at all. She said they were too old and assumed they were prepping me for boys. While that was not the case, there was no convincing Grandma Reese. One summer evening I ran back to the house to use the restroom and I invited Niecy and Mika in with me. Grandma Reese had a tendency to be rude and say whatever it was she was thinking. As the two stood at the living room stairs waiting for me, Grandma Reese said "You better get those girls with them big ass titties out of my house. You're already fast and that's exactly why!" As embarrassed as I was, the girls laughed it off and left respectfully. Regardless of what Grandma Reese or anyone thought of them, they were like my big sisters. I grew to love them and hoped they would always be around.

94th was no longer a fun place to be in the summer. Needless to say my being with the sisters more, made Peaches my new found enemy. Tension between she and Travis began to grow which led to fighting between her and my family. The summer was ending but what type of block would 94th be without a memorable moment? It was the close of summer, Peaches and Travis got into a huge physical fight. While I don't remember the details, I do remember Peaches coming down to the house to finish the job. Peaches began to curse my Grandma Reese and it really upset some members of my family. My family was the type of family that fought amongst each other but when one of them was threatened by an outsider, they would develop the deadliest tag team. I'm not sure how the fight ended but I know it involved my mom and Aunt Cara. Nevertheless, it changed the relationship between my family and Peaches' family for a long time.

It was fall of 1992. Brittany and I left "Southside Boogie" and transferred to a school closer to the southwest side of the city. For the sake of names, we'll call this school, "Southwest Uppity." It was extremely hard to leave my girls especially Megan and Lucky. I missed them all summer and now I couldn't see them during school? Anyhow, like children do, Brittany and I adjusted. Going on 94th during the school year was quiet. I didn't see anyone anymore and the nature of our friendships began to change. The block still felt like an extended family but something was changing, I was changing. Changing schools allowed me to be a different person. If I could find one word to describe the school environment, it would definitely be "White." The teachers were White and most of the students were White. I wasn't worried about making friends but getting the boys to notice me was still difficult. I remember my first day, I overheard another classmate say "ewww, I don't like that black girl, she look like a duck." The other children laughed and it did nothing but piss me off. I stood up and cursed at him as if I invented the words myself. He looked as if he'd seen a ghost; nonetheless I had forever earned my respect. No one at the new school really knew my background. One could tell that these kids were different from the ones I grew up with on 94th. Most of them were nice and others were what I like to call "wanna be's." As time went on I adjusted to the change but there was one thing that happened that changed the way I functioned at this new school forever. One day, I was sitting in the class room and in walked this new student. The teacher began to introduce her but to me, she didn't need an introduction because it was one of my best friends from "Southside Boogie" . . . Lucky. I was so happy to see her for she was with me again. It was at that moment, I believed I could survive there. I began to engage in social activities and meet other people. I grew close to other girls as well. I knew they genuinely liked me but it seemed they were closer with Lucky and so I fit in. Time went on and I survived my first year in "uppity town." I participated in the young authors contest, was a part of music and danced in a talent show. For some reason it seemed boys made everything better. I had the hugest crush on an upper classman named Bryce. To me, he was the most handsome thing since Al B Sure. He was an athlete for the southwest uppity school, probably too old for me to be looking at but I couldn't keep my eyes off him. However, his girlfriend made sure I did. Her name was E. She was the typical light skinned, long legs, long hair, cheerleader type that most boys wanted in the 90's. She had bright cherry red lips that Bryce really seemed to like. I saw them kiss in the hallway one day and I almost died. I will never forget the day I came to school wearing bright red lipstick. I stole it from my mom and just knew it would get Bryce's attention. The teachers sure noticed it. That afternoon, I was roaming the hall, hoping that Bryce would see me. It was time for me to get to my class and I must have forgotten to take the lipstick off because once I entered the classroom, the teacher yelled, "Cori, you are not grown and this is not a bar. Please take off that lipstick." The class laughed and so did I. For some reason, it always took more than a public announcement for me to get embarrassed. I did as she instructed and went on with my day. I don't think Bryce ever noticed me and I had to be ok with that because it was time to move on.

"Southwest Uppity" wasn't the most exciting place for me. I imagine it was because this was my first time being around White people. One teacher in particular, I could've definitely gone through life without meeting and I'll call her Ms. Meanie. Ms. Meanie was just that. She didn't seem to like children and most of all, she didn't seem to like me. I didn't realize how cenacle, this was back then but when the children would get out of control, she would get our attention by saying, "Act your age and not your color." Now I've heard of act your age and not your shoe size but not your color? I immediately told Patsi what she said and that's when I was given my first lesson on what it meant for me to Black in America. Although I didn't understand it, I was told that White people didn't like us. I was also told that they weren't our friend and to stay away from them. I didn't want to believe that the only reason Whites didn't like Blacks was because of their skin color. We must have done something to them to make them feel this way. Let Mae tell it, we did absolutely nothing but breathe and that's why she needed to save our souls with the Karan. One day I asked Mae, "If Whites don't like Blacks because of their skin color, then why don't Blacks like me? I'm Black too." She responded "Girl I don't know, some people are just crazy." The concept seemed too deep for me at the time but it was a question that I really wanted an answer to. Little did I know, only experience could answer that for me.

Chapter 4

Turning Point

I WATCHED PATSI STRUGGLE TO avoid going back to 94th. She continued to work full time. She and Carl were still together and their toxic relationship became more and more nerve wrecking to me every day. To cope, I listened to music. I sung to myself all the time as I stood in the mirror and imagined that all the stuffed animals on my bed were millions of people watching me. Silly I know, but it was the only time I felt important. Coincidentally, Niecy moved down the street from me so I was able to see her without going on 94th. I didn't go on 94th as much as I use to because I was getting older and Patsi was allowing me to stay at home alone. Chubb and I were no longer the puppy love sweethearts we once were and as a matter of fact, he found a new love. She apparently swooped in once we moved off the block and those two apparently had real love. None of that really mattered to me because I on the other hand had bigger problems and they included learning who I was and surviving my mother. With moving all the time it was hard to learn who I was and how I affected others. I was going to sixth grade soon and all I knew of myself was that I had an attitude and a way with the boys. No one could dare say anything to me and this would be the year that would change my life forever.

Patsi received a nice settlement so we left the city and relocated to the suburbs. She thought it was a better place for us, especially me since I couldn't stop fighting. She bought a house in the suburbs. She bought a new car, increased our eating out, turned the basement into a beauty shop and spiced up her wardrobe. Unfortunately, with moving comes another transfer of schools. I was now attending school in south suburbia and the first day of school would be the day that Cori officially left the building. I can't remember my teachers name but I do remember seeing two familiar faces, Megan and Kyla. Kyla and I met when I was maybe 6 years of age. It was funny to see her and Megan bicker about who knew me first. Nevertheless, I felt honored and excited to see Megan again. Just as I had seen Lucky back at "Southwest Uppity," I knew that she and Megan would be the friends I'd have forever. As we gathered in the building from outside, Megan went to her class room and I headed to mine. "Have a seat." the teacher nicely requested. "I am going to call names and when I'm done, if your name hasn't been called, raise your hand." About 25 names later, I didn't hear mine or anything that sound like Cori, so I raised my hand. "What's your name, sweetheart?" she asked. "Cori," I replied. She asked for a last name and birth date. When I gave her the information, she said, "I have someone with your birth date and last name but the first name isn't Cori." Confused and scared, I asked her what the first name was and she replied, "Nya." I believe she thought I was being defiant because I told her "Nya" wasn't my name. To avoid arguing with a child, she asked me what I preferred to be called. I politely responded, "B."

Later that evening I eagerly told Patsi what happened. I just knew she would say that there was some kind of mistake and she would fix it first thing in the morning. Unfortunately, when one drinks all the time, it's really easy to forget to tell your daughter that you changed her name. "I thought that would've happened a long time ago," she said as she held a cigarette in one hand and a cocktail glass in the other. "Your trifling ass daddy named you after one of his hoes and I wasn't having that shit." Patsi said she saw a Polaroid of a woman who clearly forgot to put on her clothes. The inscription read, "To Charles, love Cori". One could tell that Patsi was still hurt about this incident, whether she moved on with Carl or not. I don't remember feeling any pain, just numbness. I believe I was more worried about how to tell everyone who knew me as Cori to now call me Nya. I decided not to worry about it. I allowed everyone to call me B as I instructed the teacher to do earlier that day.

Time went on and I was getting use to living in what we called the "burbs." Brittany and I shared a room again and that did absolutely nothing for our relationship. She was messy, annoying and sucked her thumb way too much. I think the only time we bonded was when we both felt hurt by Patsi. It was very quiet in our new town. The only noises I recall were the sounds of the train tracks behind us and the yelling and screaming Patsi often did. As Patsi's money increased so did the drinking and fighting. She and Carl were not getting along; I knew it, the neighbors knew it and the police knew it. I often drowned out the sound by listening to music, singing or finding a boy to focus on. I spent most of the summer going back and forth between the suburbs and the city. Grandma Reese and the rest of the family were still there. I stayed into arguments with Peaches and the new girls on the block, who apparently was given the "run-down" about me prior to meeting me. So now I had new enemies and boy was this going to be fun. Niecy and Mika were still around and ready to fight for me. Summer 1993, Peaches became close to a girl named Shaunie. Shaunie was a few years older than I was and didn't know much about me but she clearly hated me. One afternoon, Mika and I were talking as we walked up and down 94th. From a distance, we noticed Niecy standing at the corner of 93rd, talking with Shaunie. Mika was the type of girl that didn't make peace and once you bothered someone that she considered family, you would forever be on her radar. I noticed the look in Mika's eyes as she tried to make out who Niecy was talking to. I imagined, she figured it out because she screamed out, "Niecy, hold that bitch!" Before I knew it, Mika was running after Shaunie. Not knowing what Mika was capable of, Shaunie ran away. Niecy did make attempts to hold her but it all happened so fast that Shaunie got away. I can only imagine what Mika would've done had she got her hands on Shaunie. However, I was only on the block to visit and didn't need the extra drama. I eventually stopped visiting 94th because I was beginning to have my own drama in my new town.

My social skills probably weren't always the best because with unstable home life, comes attitude. Growing up on 94th helped me develop courage and taught me the value of loyalty. A huge part of my social world was determining who I was. I kept a smile on my face. I remember taking initiative and sometimes that included doing the things that no one else wanted to do or saying the things no one else wanted to say but may have been thinking. I had the strength and weakness of keeping in touch with people, whether they deserved to be in touch with me or not. I continued to keep all the friends I had from "Southside Boogie" as well as those from 94th. It seemed harder for me to keep up with everyone from "Southwest Uppity" so I stopped reaching out. I discovered that my life in the suburbs would bring a lifetime of friends and an imprint on my identity forever.

It was now August of 1993, I felt myself going through so many changes. I became a victim of menstruation. I wanted more privacy. I kept my door closed with the radio turned up and the cordless phone somewhere close by. Connie was my closest friend at the time so we spent a lot of time between my house and hers, roaming the streets and meeting people. I wanted to deny the idea that this menstrual cycle was making me "boy crazy". No matter where I turned, there was some boy who was just "oh so fine". The attention they gave became addictive. They talked to me, seemed interested in what I thought and how I felt. For the wrong reasons, I became consumed with thoughts of being a girlfriend. However, I had been given the speech about boys being trouble a million times and while no one ever bothered to tell me why, I really tried to keep myself distracted.

During the school week, I found myself doing a lot to keep busy and stay out of the house. I tried out for volleyball and became very good at it. I'm not sure if I needed to channel anger or learn a new way to deal. Nevertheless, it taught me discipline. So much discipline that I avoided my first fight. The first week of school went by and because my school was co-ed, it was difficult to deny my attraction to a boy I thought to be very handsome. I mentioned to someone that I thought he was cute. Little did I know, he had a girlfriend that didn't like my "checking him out." I would soon learn the unwritten rule that in middle school it is forbidden to find another girl's boyfriend cute.

In the first few weeks at Jr. High, I met a lot of new friends. Some didn't like me because I thought I was cute (so they said) and others didn't like me because their boyfriends thought I was. My favorite group of friends were all on the volleyball team. We spent a lot of time together, conditioning, competing and most of all bonding. Many days after school during the season, the team would scrimmage. There was a spot in the gymnasium where we would wait for our team's turn to play. It was at the top of the stairs, a balcony full of blue mats, open space, a desk and a cage of volleyballs. Some of the girls laughed and talked amongst each other, while others such as myself, lied on the mats to watch below as the other teams played. Beside me was another team player. She seemed to know everybody and everybody seemed to know and respect her. She was short in height, very cute with brown skin and high cheek bones. Her demeanor was very quiet and calm, almost like the personality of a silent killer. She never really said much to me. I almost believed she didn't like me. September 22, 1993, she and I both were watching down below as the other girls scrimmaged. There was complete silence between the two of us until she turned and said to me, "Do you like Jimmy?" Puzzled at her question, I replied, "I don't like him but I think he's cute, is that alright with you?" I turned my head in an effort to continue watching the game and thinking "Bitch quit talking to me." I reckon she felt the vibe for she lifted up from the mat as in disbelief that I had just blew her off. She leaned forward, making sure I noticed her and said, "Well, I'm his girlfriend." Placing my head in the fold of my arms and laughing, I replied "So." It seemed my laughing affected her for she began to laugh also. Once the laughter calmed down, she said, "I did sound kind of stupid. You held your ground though, I like that. Most people would've lied about it. I like you." She introduced herself as Jackie and I'm guessing because someone told her I liked Jimmy, she already knew my name. After that day, Jackie and I became inseparable and later developed a friendship that would change my life forever.

You ever heard the phrase "guilty by association?" I sometimes believe I became "popular by association." While I never forgot about the friends I had at my previous school, we seemed to be headed in different directions. Megan and Kyla became friends with a more pure group of ladies. It seems they were being the girls they were supposed to be and I was sneaking myself into womanhood. I no longer wanted to play with dolls or jump double-dutch. I wanted to talk on the phone and hang out with girls that had real fun going on. Getting close to Jackie meant getting close to Brandy and Carly. While these were her peers and girls she developed bonds with before me, they accepted me and grew to have my back as she did.

Brandy was short in height just like Jackie. She was dark-skinned just as Jackie and I were. She had long thick hair, an asymmetric cut to be exact. Her personality was that of a firecracker and dramatic nonetheless. She liked to talk and she most definitely liked to gossip. One could tell she cared a lot about Jackie and was threatened by anyone who interfered with their closeness. Brandi and Jackie often dressed alike. They shared clothes and shoes and some believed they were related. At times I enjoyed hanging with Brandy and other times, I wanted to wring her neck. There was just something about our dynamics that didn't always allow us to get along. She seemed to lie about everything from boys who liked her to things she said or didn't say in the midst of running her mouth. Us city girls didn't do "fake and phony" and Brandy would soon meet the girl from 94th.

Just as she had with Jackie, Brandy shared an attachment to Carly. I would describe Carly as sweet, privileged and loyal. She was different from the rest of us. She had a two-parent household, access to vehicles, the latest fashions with accessories and the cutest brother a girl could have (ok, I digress). Carly was what the boys called "thick." While not the tallest, she had curves and all the traits the high school boys liked such as long hair, light skin and confidence. Although her socioeconomic status seemed higher than ours, she never treated us differently. She shared what she had and opened her doors when we needed her to. I loved her as I loved Jackie and Brandy. They were more than my friends, they were my sisters but life would soon test that and two of us would one day no longer be friends.

One of the things that made my friendship with Jackie, Brandy and Carly solid was our ability to have each other's back. There weren't many times an "outsider" could come between us. When one of us fought, we all fought and that seemed to be the silent understanding among us. I will never forget the day, the seventh grade class decided to jump me in a fight. As I stated earlier, I wasn't very popular with the girls. I somehow take responsibility for that in which I had a huge mouth that often said "I'm bad and you're not so fuck you and fuck you too." I wasn't afraid to tell someone how I felt about them. In hindsight it wasn't the smartest thing to do but appropriate for my age and lifestyle. You remember Kyla, the young lady I reconnected with back in the first school from the burbs, who argued with Megan over who knew me first? Unfortunately, we grew apart and word got around that I had a strong dislike of her presence. I didn't think this was a shocker considering how we treated each other but for some reason, the 7th grade girls seemed quite surprised. November 11, 1993, I prepared to play in a volleyball tournament in Wisconsin so a few teammates and I decided to walk to the neighborhood liquor store for snacks to eat on the way there. As I turn the corner on the block, I heard a crowd behind me. "Fuck that bitch," someone shouted from the crowd. "Whoop her ass," another yelled. I turned to see who the crowd was talking to and clearly it was me. Like my bad ass always did, I stopped and turned to face them. Kyla walked towards me and said, "I heard you don't like me, B." Laughing, I replied "I don't, now what?" It was at that moment, I saw Kyla rush towards me but not by any force of her own. It seemed someone standing behind Kyla pushed her into me in an effort to jumpstart the fight. In the 90's, fights usually started when the instigator said "Whoever's the baddest person hit my hand." It was almost as confirming as a minister saying, "I now pronounce you husband and wife." In this case the instigator pushed her into me, making her the baddest person and I had to do something about that. There we were, fighting and there I was, in my volleyball uniform, dressed to play and ramming this child's head against a wooden door. The crowd was yelling, I felt multiple hands hitting me from behind but I could only focus on Kyla. I would say it was an exaggeration to feel the entire 7th grade hitting me but it really wasn't. I overheard someone in the crowd yell, "throw her in the street." Feeling the combination locks against my scalp, my hair being pulled and what appeared to be hairspray being sprayed in my face, I became numb yet I refused to let Kyla go. Before I knew it, the pressure on my back began to lighten and the noise behind me became less. It seemed my dream team had arrived, smacking girls one by one and pulling them off of me. It was like a heroic scene in a ninja movie. You know the part where you think the underdog is about to die but someone comes to save the day? Carly, Jackie and

Brandy were my saviors and to this day, I have no clue how they heard I was being beaten, but I was happy they decided to show up. Before long, the police arrived and we all were arrested. By this time, I had been in so many fights that the police new me on a first name basis. I believe this officer had grown tired of me for he didn't ask me any questions. He threw me in the back of his car and slammed the door as if his only daughter had disgraced him. My punishment as usual was to either spend Saturday mornings detailing police cars or spend time in Juvenile Detention. Tired of the mini lock ups, I opted for car detailing.

Patsi was not happy that the same things that happened on 94th were occurring in the suburbs. Her yelling and screaming rang in my ears, leaving an everlasting tone. While she knew I had a "big mouth" and provoked many people, she also felt that girls were jealous of me. Patsi had a way of taking credit for things when they clearly had nothing to do with her. "Those bitches don't know your momma. I paid for those clothes. I do your hair, they must want to fight me," Patsi screamed. Patsi called a mandatory meeting with all the girls and their parents. Don't ask me how she "punked" all the parents into coming. It wasn't difficult for Jackie, Carly and Brandy to identify who they ambushed. I will never forget the day Patsi had the meeting. One by one, the girls came to my house with their parents. I think Patsi scared the living flesh out of them with her intimidating frown and police questioning. As I sat there hearing the girls talk about why they didn't like me and why they jumped in the fight, it made me angry all over again. "She thinks she's all that," one girl said. "She talks too much," another one said and the most complimenting of all, "she thinks she's cute." Patsi wanted details. She wanted to know how I thought I was all that and how was it that everyone disliked me? It was the way I wore my hair, the way I walked, the way I talked and the way I abandoned every girl in my grade to hang with Jackie, Brandy and Carly. It was at that moment I realized that maybe my spirit was too old for my peers or maybe, just maybe, it wasn't just my mouth afterall.

Chapter 5

Boys! Boys! Boys!

THE GIRLS AND I GREW closer after my ambush. We spent a lot of time in the house just to stay out of trouble. It was getting colder out so we spent weekends dancing at a southside skating rink, hanging out in my mom's beauty shop, talking on the phone, going back and forth to 94th and the best of it all, meeting boys. I don't remember what happened to Jackie and Jimmy after that but they weren't together too much longer after we met. Jackie later began dating someone else and I began exploring a world of boys unheard of. In my preteen years, I noticed boys began to show a different interest in me; an interest that seemed to be more of a mature nature. At first I didn't quite understand it but Jr. High would sure teach me. For some reason, the boys in the suburbs seemed to have more charm than the ones in the city. It was either that or they were more subtle with what they wanted. I found myself being confused most days about how to read 'the signs.' I knew from watching television that they at least wanted a kiss or a hug. At 12, the routine was to giggle and say to your friend, "Ooh he's cute." Your friend would then yell out "Ay boy, my friend said you're cute." You then giggle and slap your friend on the shoulder and say "Why you do that?" Before you knew it, he had your number and for the next 24 hours, you held the phone hostage waiting on his call.

I accepted the fact that I was becoming "boy crazy." I had a "thing" for light-skinned boys. Based on my experience with having darker skin, I found myself developing the same attitude towards myself and other dark-skinned Blacks. Just as everyone treated me, I thought being dark was unfortunate. While I didn't understand the history of dark-skin, I knew that having it meant you were picked last, called names or even over-looked. It was a reality and when boys would tell me they thought I was pretty, I wanted to believe them and whether it was the truth or not, I accepted it. There was a type of boy that I just knew I could never get. Some of us call him the "pretty boy". Back then, most "pretty boys" were described as light-skinned, pretty eyes, nice teeth and wavy hair. It seemed they had their type of girl too and none of them looked like me.

I will never forget the first boy to see real beauty in me. He was a classmate, the first boy I dated in Jr. High and the first boy I ever thought to be handsome with dark-skin. I can't recall if other girls liked him but I sure did. His name was Conner. He had the nicest voice. One could tell his mother wouldn't let him leave the house without Vaseline to protect that flawless skin. Not that I am proud of it but I was very sneaky back then. When Patsi would go to work, I'd have tons of guests. The girls and I would invite our boyfriends over, eat and hang out until she was on her way home. December 9, 1993, as usual, the girls and I had guests. Many of them had to leave early because they wanted to beat their parents home. Conner lived down the street from me so for him, there was no rush. The house became empty and he had this "look" in his eye. Conner and I spent a lot of time hugging and kissing. We never took it any further. This day I had a feeling that he wanted to. Standing in the living room, he walked closer to me. I could always tell when he wanted to kiss me and so I pushed my face against his. There we were like two adults in a romance novel. We made our way to Patsi's room because she had a big bed. Conner was lying on top of me. I heard his belt buckle rattle as if he was trying to pull down his pants. Nervous, I joined him in pulling down my pants. Still there were no words; just a lot of heavy breathing. After a while, the kissing became boring as I knew we should be doing more. Conner begins to grind on me as if he was really into this. I'm feeling a lot of pressure and tickle against my stomach. Discomfort is all I feel. "What are we doing?" I asked. "We're doing it," he replied. "In my belly button?" I responded. "That don't feel good?" he asked. (Laughing) I replied, "No it doesn't. I don't think we're doing this right. Get up." As I requested, Tony got up. He was sweating profusely as if he had just run a marathon. I told him that we'd try again later but it was time to go because Patsi would be home soon. Needless to say, I didn't lose my virginity that day. I didn't know how to feel about that moment so after I cleaned the house, especially Patsi's room, I called the girls to discuss what happened.

Calling the girls was probably not the best thing to do. I would soon learn my first lesson in communication: don't tell anyone anything that you don't want getting back. At this particular Jr. High, all of the classes lined up around the back of the building until their teacher brought them in. If a student happened to arrive early, some of us tend to talk, jump double-dutch or stand around. It felt odd walking on school grounds the next day. People I didn't regularly talk to were running towards me and laughing hysterically, "I heard Conner put it in your belly button." As embarrassed as any 7th grader could be, I covered my face with my hands and thought, "I could go with this or run from this," so I chose to go with it. "Girl yes he did and he had the nerve to be sweating," I added. Other students started to gather around me as I told the story. I wanted to stop. My brain kept saying, "B, shut up. You are ruining this boy's reputation," but my mouth just kept moving. I watched as Conner entered the school yard. A few of our classmates ran to him just as they did me. I imagine the conversation went something like, "Ah ha, you fool, you put it in her belly button." Conner was an 8th grader so I can imagine how embarrassing it was for his peers to know that he couldn't find the vagina. I saw the anger in his eyes. He dropped his book bag and came charging at me. In shock that he was coming towards me, I froze. He tackled me like a quarter back on a Monday night. I began to punch him in his back. He wouldn't let me go. It was very clear that he wanted to hurt me and there was no way I was going to let that happen. I continued to punch him as he tried to get me on the ground. As some of the classmates watched in amusement, my girls and his friends were breaking us apart. Needless to say, Conner and I never spoke again. The students all called him the "bellybutton boy."

The year was 1994 and boys were becoming a major priority for me. I was worried that I would never develop, so I did what any feline in heat would do . . . stuffed my bra with tissue. When hanging out with the girls, we happened to meet boys every place we went. Patsi (still having no clue how fast her daughter was) relaxed my hair and cut it asymmetric. She arched my eyebrows and decided that I was ready to look like a teenager. I was turning 13 this year and Patsi cared deeply about how her girls looked. The weather was beginning to break and thank God because Chicago's winter was beginning to be a bit uncomfortable. Jackie, Carly, Brandy and I spent the rest of the school year incognito. Those three were getting ready to graduate and I was preparing myself to be stuck with girls who didn't like me. Nevertheless I was prepared and they all agreed that since high school dismissed before Jr. High, they would be there waiting for me in case I needed back-up. And boy, did I need back-up.

March 17, 1994, another boring day at school. While I continued to be academically strong and could pass my classes asleep, my people skills were just a bit challenged. I walked to my last class of the day and it was science, I recall. I walked to my seat and saw a note for me written on the desk with an eraser. It read, "B's a hoe," My first impulse was to go out into the hallway and yell "who wrote this shit" but my Spidey senses suggested that I look at the teacher's seating chart for the class prior to see who sat there. So I did and the name on the chart read, Tyeisha Sullivan. Now this came as no surprise considering I couldn't stand her or her feminine brother. I marched out of the classroom to what I believed to be her locker. I saw her standing there engaged in a conversation. I rudely interrupted by standing in between them, "I know you wrote that shit about me on the desk," I snobbingly said. "I didn't do it and if I knew who did, I definitely wouldn't tell you," Tyeisha replied. "Well bitch we'll see who tells who what after school. I'm kicking your ass," I said. "See you then, hoe," screamed Tyeisha. I walked away, heartbeat racing and blood rushing through my veins. "What did I just do?" I asked myself. I didn't know for sure that she wrote it and I just challenged her to a fight. I got another thought, "What if she kicks my ass?" Whether or not she could, there was going to be a fight and I started it so there was no way I was going to back out.

Watching the clock for 3:15, the bell finally rang. It was now around the entire school that B and Tyeisha will be fighting. Classmates are betting on who will win and who needs to win. I'm nervous because I'm thinking about getting ambushed again. However, by this time, my peers are convinced that I'm no punk and that the dream team doesn't play. As I walk out of the school towards Tyiesha and off campus ground, Jackie and Brandy are vowing not to jump in. They're whispering in my ear where to hit her and suggesting it's best for me to make the first punch. I remember convincing them that this wasn't my first fight and that I would be ok. Carly was nowhere to be found and that was probably a good thing. There Tyeisha stood with a crowd around her. I walked up to her, balled up my fist and connected it with her chin. We began to fight. It seems the first thing all of my opponents went for was my hair. Tyeisha didn't have much hair and neither did she have nails. My famous act of defense when I felt someone had too much of my hair was to grab their neck with both hands, stick my nails deep in the skin and pull. It worked every time and this time, I may have gone too far. I broke more than skin. I exposed tissue. Most children enjoyed a good fight until things became too serious. I remember a fellow classmate breaking us up. Jackie and Brandy walked me home and while it seemed Tyeisha got the best of me by the yanking of my hair, I had her skin underneath my nails. It seemed there was no winner, especially after she and her mother pressed charges. Since the fight was off school grounds, I didn't get suspended so it seemed easy to keep this fight from Patsi (that is until the police knocked on our door to take me away, AGAIN!!). One would think I was tired of detailing police cars and I wasn't tired until they made me do it for the remainder of the school year.

The next day my mother forced me to go to school. She didn't care if I had slept or not. She was clearly fed up with me and wanted me to face every consequence, natural or otherwise. I had the heaviest bags under my eyes. It seemed people were angry with me for the damage I did to the back of Tyeisha's neck. As I prepared to stand in line and wait for my teacher, here comes Carly. "B, what the fuck was you thinking? How dare you have a fight without me? Did you even know for sure if Tyeisha called you a hoe?" I imagine Jackie and Brandy filled her in. She made notice to the bags under my eyes. I told her my version of the story and as I relived that fight, I began to cry. This was the first time I had ever expressed raw emotion, vulnerability or complete sadness since Darren passed. Carly grabbed me by the arm. She hugged me and slowly walked me back to my line. I don't know what came over me that day. All

I can remember was feeling sad or maybe it was guilt from scarring what could've been an innocent person, making yet another enemy for no reason at all. I was glad school was ending. I needed another focus and school wasn't it.

My girls graduated 8ᵗʰ grade and I was very happy for them. In less than a year, we all would be in different schools. Carly was going to be attend Wildcat High; Brandy was expected to attend Falcon High; Jackie was attending Thunderbird High and I was going back to Jr. High. However, before we separated, we made certain our summer was fun. Patsi and Brandy's mother were now friends. Patsi was doing well in her salon and she was now the beautician to all my friends. My cousin Connie was visiting on the weekends and for a while there seemed to be peace. While Patsi continued to drink, it didn't seem to bother me as much. She and Carl had their good days as well as their bad but it wasn't anything I couldn't handle. I committed to giving up fights. I started to believe it wasn't very "lady-like" and if I wanted a nice boy, he probably wouldn't want a girlfriend with a record. I didn't dress very feminine these days. I wore gym shoes also known as sneakers, baggie jeans and loose fitted tops. The only reason one knew I was a girl was because of the hair. I was still underdeveloped, meaning no breasts, no booty and no hips and I'm thinking, "There's gotta be a way to get out there and prove I'm a woman." There was just one problem . . . I wasn't.

Summers in the suburbs were safe and fun. While I had only lived there two years, I noticed they always had nice activities. My favorite activity was the carnival. It started around the 4ᵗʰ of July. Some would call it fun town. I like to call it the foundation of my womanhood. Friday, July 1, 1994, my cousin Connie came to spend the weekend with me as she did many summers. Bored and tired of Patsi, Brittany and Carl, we decided to take a walk. It was a very normal yet not so safe act for pre-teens to walk the streets in the summer time. We walked and talked and somehow found ourselves at the park. As I stated earlier, Connie was very pretty and like Carly, she was what the boys desired. I liked to think of her as our "boy magnet." We sat on a railing that separated the park from the neighborhoods and while we rested, we noticed two males walking across the park. They were clearly looking for trouble as they approached us. One of them took an interest in Connie, while the other one decided that in an effort to avoid boredom, he would talk to me. I introduced myself as B and said I was 15 years old. He introduced himself as Byron and said he was 17 years old. Somehow we decided that these two strangers were our new best friends. Byron appeared to be 5'11 in height. He had skin the color of caramel, a box hair cut and wore a polo shirt with khaki shorts. Prematurely we decided to take a walk with them and get to know them a little better. I imagine it got too hot outside because they asked if wanted to come in their house for cool air and something to drink. With little to know hesitation, we agreed.

After walking around their house and getting the grand tour, we ended up in a bedroom. The two asked us how we felt about splitting up. Full of apprehension and reluctance, Connie and I replied "I guess." As we agreed, Connie went into the other room with her new friend and I decided to stay with Byron. Not sure of what would happen next, Byron closed the door and began to kiss me. Seeing as though I had been down this road before, I eased up a little and thought to myself "I can do this." I imagine the kissing turned him on for he began to take down his pants. I remember wearing a skirt this day so he pulled mine up. Considering, my first experience I saw nothing wrong with this picture. It seemed things were going the way they were supposed to. I proceeded to let him touch me, kiss me and say things to me that I had never heard before. He stood over me wearing a white pair of Fruit of the Looms and asked, "Do you see what you did to me?" Not knowing at the time that he was speaking of having a hard on, I responded, "I'm sorry, what did I do?" He asked me to lay back and like he was a doctor, I followed instruction. He pulled down my panties, lied on top of me again and before I knew it, I was experiencing the worst pain of my life. I screamed "Ouch" as I felt an unpleasant pressure. Byron jumped up and yelled, "Oh no, I think I just popped your cherry! You have to go!"

Chapter 6

Missing Innocence

I LOOKED DOWN AND I was hysterical for there was blood on the sheets and in between my legs. I started calling on God. "Oh God, Oh God," I repeated. I was horrified. I just knew I heard the angels calling. Connie and Byron's friend must have heard us from the other room because they began to knock on the door in an effort to get in. I heard Connie on the other side yelling, "B, are you ok? Boy if you hurt my cousin, I am going to kick your ass!" Byron continued to ignore them and make very strong attempts to explain to me what he had just done. He seemed disappointed and frightened. He handed me a towel from nearby and suggested that I clean up the mess. He then kneeled down in front of me and asked, "Were you a virgin? Have you ever had sex?" "No, I've never had sex." I told him. He seemed shaken up. He patted me on my leg and said, "I'm sorry. I'm so sorry. I need to walk you back to the park." I still didn't understand why Byron was apologizing. I imagine he believed he had hurt me in some way. Connie and his friend were still on the other side of the door interested to know what just happened. I yelled to Connie that I was alright and that we would be leaving soon. I put on my panties, I fixed my skirt and Byron finally opened the bedroom door. Connie came barging in like she was the police looking around for evidence. "What happened B? What happened? What did he do to you?" She was loud and I remember her dramatic entrance making me feel even more nervous. I knew she was concerned and scared of the unknown. I reassured her that I was fine and would tell her what happened on our way back to the park.

As promised, Byron and his friend walked Connie and I back to the park. We walked in complete and utter silence. I held my head down most of the way, counting the cracks in the sidewalk. Connie was to the left of me with her arms wrapped around my shoulders. I believe she had an idea about what happened but she hadn't said anything yet. We weren't too far from where the boys found us so once we reached our destination, Byron gave me a kiss and said he'd see me later. We exchanged phone numbers and he left. I later told Connie what happened and I believe she was more in shock than I was. She shared what went through her mind as she heard me chanting, "Oh my God." I didn't know what to do and I definitely knew I wasn't telling anyone. By this time, no one had ever talked to me about what to do if I was ever faced with sex. Everything I knew, I learned from television and peers. It was never apparent that the girls were having sex because we only talked about kissing. Nevertheless, Connie and I vowed to keep this to ourselves and I went on with my day as if nothing happened.

Connie and I sat at the park for a little while. It was kind of painful for me to walk and I didn't want to bring attention to myself. We must have sat there for an hour before I saw Byron walk back to the park with his arm around some girl. In disbelief, I walk up to him and ask, "Byron, who is this?" The other girl stepped back from underneath his arm and said to him, "Do you know her?" Byron responded with "Naw I don't, she's just some girl who like me." Apparently hurt and confused by his response, I began to tear. "How could you say that after what you did to me?" I cried. Connie grabbed my arm, pulling me in the opposite direction, "Don't cry B, let's go home." I followed her to avoid punching him. He walked away without a care and willing to stick to the story that we never met. I don't know what felt worst, a stranger taking my virginity or a boy taking my virginity then acting like we never met. I never saw Byron again after that and I didn't want to. I believed I had bigger problems and this park was just the beginning.

Needless to say, I ended up telling Jackie what happened. One would think she wanted to find Byron and hurt him but noooo, she wanted to go to the park and meet more guys. It seemed I was the only one traumatized by what happened and late on losing my virginity. I didn't quite get the sympathy I expected. Saturday, July 2, 1994, Connie went home earlier that morning and Jackie's mom dropped her off at my house. The carnival was still going on and Jackie was interested in helping me get over my tragedy. "Let's go to the carnival and meet some more people," she said. I decided to get dressed and this time I chose not to wear a skirt. I am still successfully wearing the asymmetric hair cut that looked best when worn in a wrap. Patsi vowed never to do my hair again so I mastered the technique of keeping it together on my own. I put on my pink silk short set with the cutest sandals, stuck in my Tazmanian Devil gold plated earrings and left. We must have arrived at the carnival pretty early because it was still day time. Jackie was determined to make me feel better so she spotted two boys hanging out by one of the rides. They both were very handsome. Unlike me, Jackie had this thing for dark-skinned boys. She melted for muscles and a pretty smile. I imagine they noticed us too for they began to walk towards us. They introduced themselves as cousins named Doc and Luke. Doc was clearly interested in Jackie and he was definitely her type. He was tall and had smooth dark brown skin. He had a body of a God and it certainly made Jackie smile. He was a gentleman in the way he spoke and his demeanor. I think her day had been made.

Just as Doc did with Jackie, Luke took an interest in me. I didn't get the vibe that it was due to boredom or obligation. I truly believe he thought I was gorgeous. Why do I believe that you ask? Well because he told me so. Luke wasn't as tall as Doc but he was so fine. He had all of his teeth, the most handsome smile, the freshest hair cut and the deepest voice that hummed to me. He wasn't light skinned but he was lighter than I was and that's all that mattered. Being a gentleman must have run in their family because Luke was just as charming as Doc (if not more). We walked around the carnival for a little while, exchanging information and getting to know one another. Luke told me he was 16 years old and attended Falcon High School. Not learning from the last incident, I told him that I was 15 and a sophomore at Thunderbird High. Since Jackie was going there, it was the most realistic lie I could come up with. He seemed pleased and relieved that I was of age and all the time I'm thinking to myself "damn liar, shame on me." Nevertheless, he didn't try to undress me or invite me back to his house so this was going well. Later that evening, Doc and Luke had somewhere to be so they left the carnival. We made plans to see each other again but before that happened, Jackie and I had more boys to meet.

It is now night time and the carnival was getting more and more crowded. Patsi trusted me beyond her wildest imagination and as long as I brought home A's, there was no way she could prove otherwise. I imagine it was around 9pm and Jackie and I were thinking of making our way back home. As we attempted to exit the park, in walks this mob of guys, dressed in matching black t-shirts with a liquor logo on the front. They appeared to be handing out flyers to a picnic. Of course they caught our attention because they were all too handsome to ignore. One walks up to Jackie, hands her a flyer and gives her a kiss. He then walks over to me, hand me a flyer and kisses me too. He proceeded to walk away but then he turned back around, grabbed me and said, "That taste good, can I have another one?" Shocked at his ambition and lack of boundaries, I gave him another kiss. We began to have conversation about my name, who I was, where I lived and that tricky question, my age. He introduced himself as William. "Ya know you're really pretty B. Do you have a man?" He asked. With the most flattered giggle, I responded, "No." He held on to me for the rest of that night. We talked and we kissed, while Jackie took a liking to his friend Chad. Me and William's chemistry was amazing. I never felt so attached to a stranger in my life. Unfortunately, as I did with Luke, I lied to William about how old I was, accept this time I was 16. There was no way I could turn him away. He smelled so good and was the "pretty boy" I always dreamed of. William had the prettiest smile. He had a grade of wavy thick hair, smooth skin and could pass for someone from India. I was in disbelief that he thought I was beautiful and whether truth or a lie, I accepted it.

I knew all my lying in a small town in the suburbs would soon catch up to me, just not that night. As William held me from behind, his arms wrapped around my tiny waist, a neighbor of mine spotted me and asked if she could talk to me for a second. I turned to William and asked to be excused. It didn't seem like William knew who she was because they didn't greet each other. My neighbor was a sophomore in high school at the time. She attended Thundercat High School and apparently knew a lot about many people, especially William. I followed her to a space behind one of the rides and she said, "B, do you know how old he is? You are going too far. He's 19 years old and has a girlfriend. You need to leave him alone now!" For her and me not to be friends, she sure as hell had an interest in what I was doing. I asked her how she knew so much and she said her best friend dated his cousin. "I like him. He thinks I'm pretty so please don't mess this up for me and please don't tell him how old I really am." I begged. She agreed to keep it to herself but that seemed too good to be true. I walked away from her, rolling my eyes at how nosey she was and made my way back to William. He offered to drop me and Jackie off at home and so I agreed. We talked on the way to my house. I gave him my number and prayed he'd see me again. It was as if I had died and gone to heaven. I thought to myself, "Two handsome guys in one day after all the trauma I had?" I was sure I had a guardian angel and no one could tell me otherwise.

Jackie and I talked all night and all morning about our day the carnival. I began spending time with and talking to both Luke and William on a regular basis. William definitely seemed more advance than any guy I had ever met. His conversation seemed to always be about sex and whether or not I ever did it orally. I didn't know what oral sex was at the time so I played along as if I had. Still lying and praying for more time, I continued to act older than I really was. I became addicted to older guys and there was no way I would even look at someone my age. Having a ride, access to money, charm and the ability to learn something became my motivation. I enjoyed William picking me up in his 5.0 Mustang. I enjoyed listening to him speak and most of all I enjoyed the way he made me feel. He noticed me and just like Luke, thought my *black* was beautiful. Still horrified from the first incident, I still hadn't engaged in any sexual activity. William and I talked a lot about sex but nothing ever happened.

The school year was approaching and I was preparing myself to start a world without my girls. While I spent most of the summer with Connie and Jackie, Carly and Brandy were well informed on my behaviors. A few weeks passed since I met William and Luke. I was somehow convinced that they both were my boyfriends. Thursday, July 21, 1994, the phone rang as I sat downstairs in Patsi's living room. It was William. He always called me "darling" in the calmest way. "How are you darling?" he asked. "I am doing good, what's up?" I replied. "You wouldn't lie to me would you?" William asked. My heart fell to my stomach as I knew what he was getting at. "Naw, I wouldn't lie to you, why do you ask?" I should've received an award for bullshitting because clearly, there goes another lie. "How old are you?" he asked. I'm thinking to myself, "Tell the truth B. Tell the truth." Instead I said, "I'm 16." Where is this coming from?" There was something about the tone in William's voice that said "Bitch I could choke you, now tell me the truth." Still calm but firm he said, "I'm going to ask you one more time, how old are you?" I gave in and said, "13." He took a deep breath and said, "I can't fuck with you anymore. Are you trying to get me in some kind of trouble? Don't call me anymore!" There it was, that same feeling I had when Byron dismissed me, accept this one was stronger. I liked William and wanted to be around him all the time. I wasn't letting him go that easy and I meant it. For days, I would call and he wouldn't answer. I cried to Connie and the girls about what to do. Jackie continued to see Chad and tried to get him to make William talk to me but he was not giving in.

A few weeks had gone by and still William wasn't speaking to me. I began spending more time with Luke and it was almost as if we were a real couple. I thought about William all the time but I had somebody who wanted to be with me and I couldn't ignore that. Wednesday, August 3, 1994, Jackie and I went to visit Doc and Luke. Most parents worked during the day so if we wanted to hang out, business hours were the best time to do so. Out of all the hanging out we did, Luke and I still weren't sexually active. We often kissed, held each other while watching a movie but nothing more. However, this day, that would all change. Usually when Jackie and I went to visit, we'd hang out as a group watching rapping Rap City or YO MTV Raps. Luke was into music and he enjoyed listening to people rhyme. Jackie and I thought we could sing so we decided to put on a show for "the fellas." We stood outside the bedroom door as we sung Mary J Blige's, 'Love No Limit.' They must have thought it was cute because Luke became a little frisky. We made our way to a bedroom that had an adult atmosphere. It reminded me of Patsi's room with the smell of perfume, a closet full of clothes and television only adults could watch. It had a big bed with curtains and matching white dressers. Luke asked me to relax and sit on top of him and without hesitation, I did. I leaned over to kiss him and as usual, his kisses tasted like honey. I decide to take things a little further and unbutton his pants. "What are you doing?" he asked. "I'm trying to see what you're working with," I replied. I heard the sound of laughter outside the bedroom door. It was at that moment, Jackie opened the door, falling to the floor, laughing hysterically as if she stood outside listening the entire time. "What are you doing Jackie?" I asked with a smile on my face. Luke must have been uncomfortable because he covered himself quickly and asked her to get out. Jackie laughed her way out of the room as Luke got up to lock the door. I thought it was rather funny but Luke didn't seem to be one for many games. I changed his focus with another kiss as we made our way back to the bed. I took off my pants, positioned myself on top of him, still at ease and in control. He was very gentle with me and didn't force me to do anything I wasn't ready to do. It didn't hurt like it did before, in fact if felt amazing. While our bodies connected so did our souls and I just knew he'd be in my life forever. It no longer mattered what happened with Byron. I felt it was time to let that go. I became someone different. I had a new attitude and I owed it all to Luke.

Chapter 7
GOING AWAY

T HERE'S A SAYING THAT, "ADULTS are innocent through a child's eyes." The older I became the more adults seemed flawed. I have reason to believe a lot of my sneaky behaviors were becoming clearer to Patsi. The boys with the deep voices were calling the house and whenever she and Brittany visited 94th, I opted not to go. Everything in my life seemed important and to me, nothing else was worth dealing with. Patsi's drinking became more and more annoying. I'm not certain what problems she and Carl were having but it was definitely having an effect on the way she lived her life. Sometimes when people are going through changes that they can't properly address, it comes out in other ways. According to Freud's Psychoanalytic Theory, defense mechanisms can play a major part in how many people cope. Many of the defenses are normal and it is expected that healthy individuals will experience one or more in their lifetime. Freud would say that Patsi's favorite defense was displacement. Displacement is a defense mechanism that shifts sexual or aggressive impulses to a more acceptable or less threatening target . . . in this case, that target was ME. While I've never been a victim of sexual aggression, it seemed verbal and emotional abuse was very prevalent in my household. Patsi was a violent drunk and cursing seemed to be her first language. Sometimes the things that came out of her mouth would make a mud wrestler feel clean. I felt helpless sometimes. It seemed there was nothing I could do every time I was called a "bitch" or a "whore" and let's not forget the infamous "You won't amount to shit" line. It didn't appear that Brittany had the same issues for she was a protected class due to her young age. However, I managed the best way I knew how and most of the time, it involved the opposite sex.

With all the drama going on at home, I continued to see Luke and stalk William. The school year began and I wasn't seeing the girls as much. Jackie and I talked often and visited when we could. Connie came to visit on the weekends and I tried to get to know the girls in my neighborhood. Many of them were cool and I actually would call some of them good friends. However, nothing came close to the way I felt when I was hugged or kissed by someone who wasn't obligated to do so. August 10, 1994, Jackie was visiting Chad after school and it was brought to my attention that William would be visiting also. I had this bright idea that since William refused to talk to me over the phone, I was going to show up at Chad's and *make* him talk to me. When I arrived at the house, I sat with Chad and Jackie at the dining room table. William eventually shows up and seems upset that Chad didn't tell him what was going on. My attempts to speak to him at first seemed useless. He still wasn't hearing me. I begged, pleaded, apologized over and over again. I believe at some point I got through to him because he finally looked at me as I spoke. However, he still didn't agree see me frustrated that he had been ambushed.

Thursday, August 11, 1994, my family and I were getting ready for a trip to Birmingham. As I packed my things in the car, Patsi yelled from the window that I had a phone call. I rushed to grab the phone and catching my breath, I said, "Hello." "Hello darling," he says. I remember having a smile bigger than a kid in a candy store. I silently screamed on the other end as if I was the 10th caller, winning a shopping spree from WGCI. "Hey," I responded. His tone low and mellow, he says, "I thought about what you said and I do miss you. I can't stop thinking about you and there's just something telling me, not to leave you alone." William's voice melted my heart through my ears. He had an effect on me that was unheard of. He asked if he could stop by. I informed him that I would be leaving to go out of town and if he were to come, it would have to be soon. William arrived at my home shortly before we pulled off. I learned a long time ago that if I wanted to perform an act that was meant to be sneaky, to do it in plain sight; that way onlookers won't notice how wrong it is. With that being said, I walked out to meet William as he parked in front of the house. Words cannot describe how happy I was to see his face. With Warren G's, "This DJ" playing in the background, he looked at me and told me I was 'something else'. I laughed but then the conversation quickly became serious. In his calm, but deep and soothing voice he said, "I agree to see you as long as you agree to keep it between us." It took no thought or time on my part to agree to his terms. I didn't ask any questions and to have him jeopardize his name and image *all for me*, made this a relationship I declared to take serious.

After my family and I spent time in Birmingham, I planned to meet William at his house. As I attempted to plan our date, I experienced the first shocker of many to come. I'm sure with William being so handsome and all, handling the women may have been routine for his mom. She often seemed warm when I called and whether or not she knew my age, she never asked me anything other than my name. August 17, 1994, as I did every day, I called William. His mom answered and told me that he wasn't home. Most people would've stopped it there and took a message but not her. One could tell that she was happy about something and wanted to either share the news or wanted me to know she was tired of me calling. "His girlfriend had the baby, he's at the hospital." She told me as if I already knew or at least I should've known. I think I stopped breathing. I immediately had a flashback of my neighbor telling me he had a girlfriend but I didn't remember her saying she was pregnant. I felt powerless over the situation because I agreed to be a secret which meant, he could do whatever he wished while I played invisible. I continued to call and finally he returned the favor. He explained his girlfriend, except it wasn't an explanation; it was more like a confirmation. Being young I had no clue what I was getting myself into and neither did I have the jurisdiction to ask him to love *only* me. All I knew was that I wanted him and probably would turn the cheek on anything he did in order to have him.

Thursday, September 1, 1994, William picked me up from my house and like always, I felt like a woman when I sat beside him. Sometimes he made me nervous and sometimes there were insecurities. I didn't feel pretty enough and I definitely hadn't given him what his girlfriend had so this day I asked, "Why me?" and "What did he have to gain by dating a 13 year old." Nevertheless, I wasn't going to ask those questions out loud and I definitely didn't want to ruin the moment.

We finally made it to William's house. It seemed he still lived with his mom. Their home was nicely decorated with figures on the shelves and pictures on the wall. Outside of being in Luke's home,

I had never really enjoyed the comforts of anyone else's. William had a bedroom themed with Michael Jordan and the Chicago Bulls. His bed was twin size or maybe it was a daybed. Regardless of what type of bed it was, I was nervous and clueless about what would happen. While I had been sexually active with Luke, I wasn't sure I was ready to go there with William and he respected that. We spent time together, talking, kissing and discussing my adult actions. He seemed very curious about my amount of freedom and unhealthy desire to be with him. He tried to lecture me most of the time, telling me how much he'd ruin my life and that I needed to find someone my age. As I did with most people, I ignored him and did exactly what *I* wanted to do. Telling me "no" was something many people didn't do and it wasn't going to start with him.

Still not engaging in sex, my date with William was coming to an end. William dropped me off at Jackie's. Her mom was expected to later take me home once she returned from work. Soon my sneaky ways would catch up to me so my lying had to get better. Once I arrived at my house, I realized I was missing my house keys. I panicked as I searched for them and they were nowhere to be found. I later learned that I left them in William's car and I had to come up with the slickest way to get them back. I remember asking William to bring them by my house. While I didn't expect Patsi to be home when she did, she received my keys *and* she met William. I will never forget the day, Patsi called me while I was at Jackie's house. "Who is William and how old is he?" she asked. My heartbeat racing as I held the phone, I responded, "He's the brother of one of my friends." I could tell by her tone, she didn't believe me but for whatever reason, she accepted my answer. There was a moment of silence before she asked me the most offensive question, "B, are you having sex?" Shocked that she would even ask me something like that, I replied, "Oh no, ma that's nasty. I'm not doing that." And again, there goes another effortless lie. "Uh huh, ok" she said and hung up the phone. I dreaded going home that day but I knew she couldn't prove that William was not the brother of an unidentified friend.

Months went on and I am still seeing Luke and William. Luke and I never engaged in sex again so I assumed I was still something like a virgin. Patsi no longer trusted me because the neighbors were informing her of all my actions while she was at work. Patsi had no problems confronting me about rumors or suspicions. It seemed to be the case that as long as I continued to get straight A's, I could convince her of anything. While that was hardly true, I think Patsi had too much going on to fight the battle. She and Carl were fighting more and more. Friday, November 11, 1994, Connie came to spend the weekend with me and Brittany. It was getting late and as we hung out in our bedroom, we heard Patsi and Carl arguing. The arguing began to escalate and out of routine, I closed the bedroom door. The commotion got louder and Brittany decided to take a peek at the action. She quickly ran back in the bedroom yelling, "B, Ma said call the police. Carl just pushed her." Annoyed by their constant fighting and history of pointless calls to the police, I waved my hand and said to Brittany, "Tell *her* to call the police; I'm not getting in the middle of that." Anyone could see that Brittany wasn't happy about relaying that message because she ignored me and sat back down on her bed. Approximately five minutes went by and we heard what sounded like someone falling down the stairs. As we rushed to get up, Patsi barges in our bedroom with a gun in her hand. She had a plastic cup in her mouth, hanging on by the grip of her teeth. She pointed the gun at me, walked closer to me, just inches away from my cheek and said, "Bitch, didn't I tell you to call the police?" Connie and I yelled with fear as Brittany screamed, "No Ma, no." As Carl did, I ran past her, stumbling down the stairs to get away. Crying and barely catching my breath, I grabbed a hold of the telephone to call 911. I explained to the dispatcher and police, my version of what occurred. As much as I loved Patsi, I no longer cared about protecting her. For the first time, the truth seemed better for me to tell. Patsi was arrested and taken to Cook County Jail. Brittany and I were taken back to 94th and that would be the last time for a long time that I'd share a residence with Patsi.

Chapter 8

Changes

PATSI'S ARREST AFFECTED MANY PEOPLE in our family, especially Grandma Reese. I think many people were in disbelief that she had taken things that far. For the first time, I realized that something was truly wrong with her. She spent the next 30 days in jail. Grandma Reese took us to visit and while very sad to see her locked up, I was still afraid of her. She denied ever pulling the gun on me and in fact it seemed she repressed the entire moment. During our visits, she talked about how well she adjusted by making friends and styling hair. I could tell she still wanted to come home. I can't say she was remorseful for her action or at least it didn't seem that way. She told me and Brittany how much she missed us and would be done with Carl once she was released from jail. I never understood why Carl was the focus and not me. Nevertheless her men were always important and I had to accept that.

Before the incident with Patsi ever took place, I was still having social problems in school. My social life began to be a series of arguments with girls over boys and unpleasant stares. Brandy and I were no longer friends. Her gossiping and drama creating personality took a toll on me. Her efforts to be a friend seemed superficial for she often smiled in my face and talked about me when I wasn't around. While I lied to my mom and males to get my way, my friends could always expect loyalty from me. Outside of letting go of Brandy, Megan and I continued to be distant. She now had a different group of friends and some of them often clashed with me when it came to boys. I sometimes believed that when Megan had to choose, she chose them. I understood her position and still loved her nonetheless. The amount of time I spent with Jackie and Carly, seemed to get less and less. Between home and school, defending myself became a top priority. It seemed Patsi resented me, either for my behaviors or hers. I became the target for all her pain and it ultimately led to our distance and my not wanting to be around her. The entire family noticed our poor relationship as well as her increase in drinking. My aunt Phyllis was becoming adjusted to her own life with a new husband and daughter but couldn't stand to see me sad. Phyllis may have had other priorities but she loved her nieces and nephews as her own, especially me. Travis' mom, my Aunt Cara, seemed to have problems as well which didn't allow her to care for him either so Phyllis decided to take custody of both of us. I'm not sure why Phyllis didn't take Brittany but she and Grandma Reese had a bond that no one could break and until Patsi's release, 94th was where she stayed.

Shortly after the incident, I moved in with Phyllis. She lived on the east side of the burbs. She didn't have a lot of space but peace and quiet became more of a preference. Phyllis worked hard to live a normal life without drama so she stayed active in church. While we were all raised in church, we didn't go as often as we could have so Phyllis made sure that Travis and I would get 'saved' again. We attended the local church up the street. Phyllis strongly insisted that I become friends with more 'Godly' people and in my mind that translated to boring, judgmental and stuffy. Since I had to do something to past the time, I joined the choir. Music had always been my escape and I didn't discriminate on the style. I enjoyed singing and believed I had talent. Outside of boys, singing was the one other thing that made me feel special. The schedule for church was the worst schedule a young teen could ever have. Monday it was choir rehearsal. Wednesday I was expected to attend Bible Study. Friday was youth night and Sunday was the traditional service. Phyllis worked in the audio room and that meant being at church all day on Sunday. The best part about being with Phyllis was my new little cousin. She was a toddler at the time and was the cutest child I ever seen. I enjoyed being around her. She took my mind off a lot. She had the squeakiest voice and said my name in the funniest way. She was so pretty for she had the lightest skin, the blondest hair and the brightest cherry red lips. Her name was Hazel. Phyllis knew that caring for Hazel would keep me busy and she was convinced that I had absolutely nothing else to do. I was in charge of doing Hazel's hair, giving her baths, feeding her, playing with her and teaching her how to keep many secrets.

Phyllis' rules were very strict and didn't allow me to talk to almost anyone. She often took the house phone to work with her so that I couldn't talk to friends after school. She believed that most drama started on the phone and she wasn't willing to be bothered with it. She insisted that I transfer schools and couldn't care less about my wanting to finish Jr. High with my class. I think she knew that I had little supervision and that I often took advantage of Patsi's drunken nights. While she believed I needed a better environment, she also believed I needed better behaviors. Friday, November 18, 1994 I transferred from one Jr. High and began attending another. For the sake of names, let's call this school, "Jr. High2." My first day was very similar to the one I had at the first Jr. High; girls and their "so-called" boyfriends. I tried to do things differently at "Jr. High2." I didn't want to fight and I didn't want to make more enemies than I already had. I had to accept a lot of things and one thing I learned thus far in life was that one person couldn't please everybody and no matter what I did, someone was bound to dislike me. As I walked down the hall from the main entrance to what was called the "North Side," I heard a commotion behind me. I immediately had a flashback of my ambush in 7th grade. I focused my ears on the background noise and I gathered that some girl was accusing me of liking her boyfriend. I noticed random unfamiliar faces, checking for my expressions and finally someone with guts asked me (I can't remember who), "Do you like Nick?" I ignored them the first time but the second time they asked, I think I lost it. "I don't know who the hell Nick is so no, hell no, I don't like him!" While I said it loud enough so others could hear, the message was still passed along, distorted and with more aggression than I put into it. The girl behind me yelled "Who the fuck she talking to? I know she's not talking to me!" I always thought it was nice how girls who wanted to be tough would talk *at* the person and not *to* the person. I must have been at the school for at least an hour and all I could think was, "Oh hell no, not this shit again." It seemed "Jr. High2" was worse than the first Jr. High and my patience was tested more and more that day. I ended that day, without hitting anyone. The class had a skating party and I don't remember making a friend. I also still didn't know who in the hell Nick was.

Monday November 21, 1994, I dreaded going back to "Jr. High2" but I had no choice. I worked really hard to abide by

Phyllis' rules. She made it clear that I was not to have any fights or get suspended. I honored her rules because I really wanted to be a better person but just like Friday, Monday wasn't going to be a good day either. Classmates talked more to me this day than they did Friday. With the Thanksgiving break coming up, I was already looking forward to the week being over. Lunch time was always the most difficult at Jr. High2. It was the time where the teachers and/ or principals, pampered their favorites and shunned their worst. As I sat eating my lunch, I heard a table full of laughter behind me. Still not knowing what all the laughter was about, I ignored it and continued to eat. A classmate leaned over to me and said, "Excuse me but you have cheese on your back." My initial reaction was disbelief but when I reached back and felt the cheese, I also felt fire running through my veins. The table behind me was still laughing and I immediately no longer cared about a suspension. I wanted to stab everyone who had a smile on their face including the girl who told me. However, without a knife or an alibi, I had to let that go. I walked over to the Assistant Principal and shouted, "Some bitch threw cheese on my back and I'm about to fight." For many reasons, I clearly didn't care that this was an adult. I didn't have much respect for them either. "Excuse me young lady, you're going to have to watch that tone and that mouth, now what happened?" she asked. As I tried to calm myself down, I told her what I knew. She said she would find out who it was but in the meantime suggested that I clean the cheese off my back. Two girls walked up and offered to help me clean the stain. Both girls seemed concerned and sorry about what happened to me. However, I trusted no one and believed anyone could have done it. Not knowing who to trust, it was really nice that the girls helped me. We started to talk as we stood in the restroom cleaning cheese off the back of my sweater. I grew to like these girls and talking to them helped changed my mood from homicidal to angry. Their names were Tiffany and Natasha. Tiffany was very playful in character. She often smiled a lot and had an interest in getting close to me. She was light skinned with neck length hair. She often wore it in a ponytail that hung from the side. She dressed nice wearing name brand clothes with gold chains and earrings. Tiffany had a small gap in her teeth and very pretty slanted eyes. Like Tiffany, Natasha was put together from head to toes. She had a caramel complexion, was tall in height and wore glasses. Although she didn't have much, she too wore her hair in a ponytail. Both girls seemed loyal and sincere in their efforts to get to know me. Tiffany and I became close, so close that we began to dress alike, sit together at lunch and go by weird names like "Sugar" and "Spice." She was "Sugar" for she was believed to be the sweetest and I was "Spice" because I was often mean and "hotheaded." Natasha fit in with us most of the time and when she didn't feel like it, she kept her distance. Sometimes, Natasha found herself only communicating with me. There was something peculiar about her for she often sought attention. She would make up stories about being pregnant and gossip all the time. On many levels I understood Natasha because I felt the way she would often act. Natasha sometimes reminded me of Jackie with how protective she was of me. It was as if she didn't care about suspensions or what no one else thought and I admired her for that. Since my sweater was vandalized with cheese, Natasha had taken an interest in making sure no one else would bother me. It seemed people thought of her as "crazy" and that usually was enough to keep them away.

The year was 1995. The end of the school year was approaching and I was making progress with avoiding fights. I was doing well in school and tried to do other things to stay busy. I was still active in church and probably not getting from it what I should. Phyllis was single handedly choosing my friends and meanwhile, my life before "Jr. High2" seemed to be fading. Luke found out about my age and decided he wouldn't talk to me anymore. One of his cousins happened to be a classmate of mine at "Jr. High2." When he called to confront me, it was like déjà vu. I had never heard Luke so angry before. As sweet as he was, I think he could've found it in himself to choke me. I can still hear his voice playing in my head, "Oh hell no . . . man are you kidding me?" I know I hurt him for he had taken a genuine interest in me and without hesitation, he let me go. As much as I knew about love, I believed I loved Luke. I knew I would do more harm than good if I begged him to stay. There was a great difference between what I did to him and what I did to William. Luke actually engaged in intercourse and developed a relationship, William did not. For the first time in my life, I realized how a small lie to *me* can become a big problem for someone else. My lies were slowly catching up to me and I had to decide to give it up. I needed to be content with the person I was and be able to walk away if people could not accept me for me.

Tiffany and I became closer as friends and for some reason, she was the only one Phyllis let come and visit. I'm sure she would have allowed Jackie supervised visiting privileges but I hadn't spoken to her in a few months. Lord knows I missed her. I wanted to tell her how I was doing and hear all about her time at Thunderbird. It was becoming routine for me to get close to people and never see them again. It was as if my life was one big revolving door. Sometimes people would come back around and sometimes they wouldn't. I wanted someone who was constant and Jackie symbolized that for me. One morning as Tiffany was heading to her locker, she mentioned she had a surprise for me. Needless to say I was more than curious to know what it was because my surprises usually weren't pleasant. She handed me a note but wouldn't tell me anything about it. I opened it and could recognize that handwriting anywhere. The letter was from Jackie. I was teary eyed as I read it and wanted to question Tiffany about how, when, and where. The letter had to be almost four pages long. She told me about Thunderbird and said she missed me. She told me about her new friends and how high school had many handsome boys. She also developed a plan for how we could see each other and it involved catching Tiffany's school bus to her house. As tempting as that was, I knew Phyllis wasn't going to go for it. Phyllis had to have control of everything. Just as I thought I could give up lying, I had to come up with another one. Phyllis sometimes associated my poor behaviors with people from my past. I told her that I was going over Tiffany's house after school one day and I was very proud of myself because it was the half truth. Tiffany helped me make my way to Jackie. It was great catching up with her and even better that I now had her and Tiffany. We vowed to always keep in touch no matter what and from that point on we did.

Things were becoming very routine living with Phyllis. I grew tired of the church boys for most of them seemed really feminine. I started reaching out to William again and to my surprise, he was available. When Phyllis and her husband would go out, I would sneak William in the house through the front door. I had to bully Hazel into going "blind" and act like she didn't see anything. Sometimes we'd try to go elsewhere but the restrictions I was under made that difficult. We still weren't having intercourse and outside of my fear, our timing always seemed bad. I'm sure William had a life with other women but I couldn't worry about that. I was still too young for him and incapable of giving him what he wanted. Phyllis often talked to me about sex and told me that I would eventually meet someone who was worthy of me giving "it" to. No one knew that I had already lost my virginity so it was easy for them to believe they had time to teach me what men like William were trying to. I didn't know if I would ever get rid of my sneaky ways. I didn't know if even wanted to. All I knew was that for the first time in my life, I was at peace and didn't want it to end.

Chapter 9

STRONG ENOUGH

THERE WERE MANY SLEEPLESS NIGHTS in which I sat up thinking about my mom. I often prayed that God would make her normal and take away her alcohol use. She was amazing when she wasn't drinking but those days became far and few. She'd been out of jail for a while now and still I never considered going home. I missed her and Brittany just not all the chaos. I didn't like being called names or made to feel like I shouldn't have been born. I didn't like fighting with Brittany and being accused of jealousy. I heard that she and Carl were back together and that sometimes discouraged me from seeing her. Eventually, I began to visit Patsi on the weekends. She would ask me if I were ready to come home and I would always tell her "No". When Phyllis wasn't being strict about church, she and I spent a lot of time in the mall, doing our nails, watching movies and doing things that mothers and daughters were supposed to do. Patsi began to blame my apprehension about coming home on Phyllis. I remember her calling the house drunk accusing Phyllis of stealing her daughter. Phyllis did a great job of ignoring Patsi but she wasn't strong enough to keep ignoring her.

I completed the school year at Jr. High2 and was planning to attend Falcon. Patsi's intimidation towards Phyllis was increasing. Phyllis wasn't receptive to confrontation of any kind. It seemed when times got rough, she would pack up and move. I imagine Patsi was making things difficult for Phyllis because she started making plans to go to California. I'm not certain what really motivated Phyllis to leave but she gave me the option of coming along or staying. Patsi begged me to come home. She convinced me that things would be different and that I could have anything I wanted. She told me that she bought a new house and was no longer living on the southeast side of the burbs. She said she moved to another location, somewhere southwest and I would now have my own room. She offered to give me a phone line and let my company come to visit. She pitched a good deal and it was difficult to turn down. Patsi made it very clear that she didn't want me going to California. I believed she wanted to change and so I chose to stay. I wanted to give Patsi a chance to be the mom I prayed for her to be. I thought if all else failed, I still had my friends.

Thursday, May 30, 1995, I moved back in with Patsi. While I believe Phyllis was respectful of my decision, she didn't seem to like it. As promised, I had my own room, my own phone line and freedom. It almost seemed like she was really trying to be a better mother. Our home was beautiful and the neighborhood was quiet. She gave me space and she wanted me to like her. I believe she wanted back the time she lost and was proud to have a teenage daughter. My going to high school was the milestone in which she lost Darren and I was convinced she didn't want to lose me. I knew Patsi wanted to have a better relationship with me and as any young child would, I wanted to have one with her too. I can't admit that I ever forgot about her pointing a gun at me; that hunted me for a while. However, I was willing to try and trusted with all my heart that she was too.

After the heavy planning and debating, Phyllis finally left for California. I didn't give her the most proper goodbye because it was hard to say. Saying goodbye to Phyllis always reminded me of her visits to 94th after work. When it was time for her to go home, I always got the privilege of walking her to the bus stop. She would lean down, give me a big hug and kiss and tell me she'd see me tomorrow. I hated saying goodbye to her for a day, I couldn't imagine saying goodbye for good and so I didn't. I forced myself not to feel anything as I saw her and Hazel pull off. She brought me the last of my things and I could tell she wanted me to hug and kiss her as I did when I was younger but I pretended to be too busy. I know that hurt her feelings and while that wasn't my intention all I could think about was how *I* could best get through it. I later began to handle all my problems that way, not knowing it was the unhealthiest thing I could ever do.

I spent most of that summer adjusting to the new environment. At first it was a little difficult because Patsi's first week in Harvey, someone had stolen her car. Although it was later found a couple of blocks away, it became difficult to trust the neighbors. Patsi was upset and suspicious of it being someone who watched us move in. Nevertheless, we got passed it and began to live like it never happened. While making new ones, I still managed to hang with old friends. Tiffany and I didn't hang out as much. Natasha later told me that while at Jr. High2, it was Tiffany who threw the cheese on my back. It suddenly made sense why Natasha was so distant when she was around back then. Furthermore, I couldn't fathom being around someone who got their 'kicks' off hurting me. As a result I began to distance myself from Tiffany.

Jackie and I continued to be close. She and her mother seemed to be having their own problems so she spent a lot of time at my house. Patsi didn't appear to mind my having company. She treated all of my friends like they were her children and she never discriminated on who she felt like cursing out. One thing I really admired about Patsi was her ability to speak her mind and her level of street smarts. She never seemed to be wrong about what things could surface in life. While many of her teachings were unorthodox, they made a lot of sense. Unfortunately, she taught from hurt and vengeance and that wasn't always helpful. I knew Patsi wanted me to find love outside of my family. She often told me to find someone who wasn't like my daddy and loved me more than I loved them. It was becoming routine for Patsi to drink and vent about how much my dad hurt her. She shocked me when she told me that in an effort to get back at him, she slept with his best friend . . . Carl. She said she never planned to be with Carl as long as she had but he was there for her. Immediately my dad's distance, every argument between me and Carl and every fight between me and Patsi made sense.

Either Patsi wanted me to feel the pain she felt and get it over with or she wanted me to experience love and live her life through me. I can only imagine one of those being her reason for encouraging me to date Shawn. I will never forget the day she took me to see the house. We were driving in her Buick and she said, "B, you're going to love the house and there's this really cute boy that lives next door. He looks like he's your age." I was shocked to hear that come out of her mouth considering the problems she had with me at the other place. I reacted by laughing it off and saying, "Ma, you're crazy." It turned out that Patsi wasn't crazy at all. She was right about Shawn being handsome. He was two years older than me and had the smile and eyes of a God. He wasn't the height I preferred but he had charm and he appeared to be a young man of little words. Shawn had a side to him that seemed a mystery. He didn't always have an answer to my questions or seem genuine in his approach to things. Challenges seemed to be something I enjoyed so I began dating him. Shawn and I spent a lot of time together. I don't think his family cared too much for me for they never spoke and treated me like I was invisible. While speaking with him on the phone, I overheard his mother call me a "fast ass." While that might have been true, his family didn't hesitate to judge me or my family. This was the first time I ever met a family that behaved like they had no problems and that everyone else was beneath them. Whether they liked me or not didn't seem to have any effect on the way Shawn felt; in fact it brought us closer.

I don't think Patsi expected me and Shawn to spend so much time together. She became worried that I was losing focus on preparing for school and having sex. She often asked me, "You ain't hot and heavy, are ya?" I would roll my eyes at her and stay silent. I still couldn't admit that I was sexually active. I continued to hide behind my grades and the idea that I was "too smart" to engage in such behaviors. Approximately a month after Shawn and I began hanging out all the time, we decided to be sexually active. We often snuck and did it wherever we could; the car, the garage, his room, the closet and sometimes my basement. I really loved Shawn and for the first time, I had a boyfriend that I could be with in public. I didn't lie to him about my age or who I was. He saw Patsi for who she was and continued to come around. While it was unfortunate that I couldn't share the same experience with his family, I was happy to be with him.

It was the end of summer 1995. Shawn's parents sent him to Oklahoma and it was time for me to prepare for school. Due to my moving, I was no longer eligible to attend Falcon. While Wildcat would've been the high school choice for our town, I was told to attend Thunderbird. Thunderbird became the beginning of a new world for me. I always heard that high school would be a turning point and a place that I would never forget. People were right about that and my time at Thunderbird would definitely change my life for the best. In an effort to stay out of trouble, I tried out for every activity there was. I participated in pom-pom volleyball and choir. I met new people and was recreating my definition of friendship. Jackie was like a sister to me so what she and I had was beyond friendship. However, we began to share different taste in friends and most of the time that meant her not liking my choices and me not liking hers. Surprisingly, it didn't cause conflict between us. We decided we would respect each other's choices and accept one another for who we became. One thing that Jackie and I never changed was the ability to have each other's back.

High school was becoming very easy for me. I continued to be strong academically and socially things seemed to be going well. With Phyllis gone and things still not going well with Travis and his mother, he started living with us. He attended Thunderbird as well making my social life even better. It was nice having him around and although just my cousin, he became the brother I missed. The honeymoon phase seemed to be ending with Patsi. It appeared her problems with Carl and life increased her drinking. Brittany and I were not getting along because her stealing was out of control. If there was nothing I despised more than an imposter, it was definitely a thief. It seemed whether Brittany was guilty or not, Patsi would still accuse me of being jealous of her. I gave up trying to convince her otherwise and just began secretly smacking Brittany every time she did something to me and boy was that a bad idea. Someone could say whatever they wanted to Patsi but NO ONE was allowed to touch her Brittany. After smacking Brittany one day, I left a mark on her face. Patsi grabbed the extension cord and had the nerve to spank me with it. I believed I was too old for spankings and while I didn't fight her back, I definitely wanted to. I called Jackie, "Can you believe this bitch just whooped me?" As Jackie did with most things, she laughed. Taunting me on the other end of the phone, "Ah haaaa, your big ass just got a whoopin'." Irritated by her lack of empathy, I hung up on her and snuck to see Shawn.

I was glad things didn't quite work out with Shawn living in Oklahoma. I needed an escape and jumping out the side window to see him overnight was helpful. We seemed to be having a real relationship and ironically, something Patsi once supported became something she now hated. I couldn't tell if Patsi liked seeing me happy or not. It seemed when I would smile, she would frown. When things were bad at home, school and friends became my outlet. It was where I had the most fun and the most peace. I took advantage of the dances and athletic games. I opened myself up to new things and started having experiences I believe Patsi always wanted to share.

Like many relationships, they appear to look better on the outside. Dealing with Shawn started to come with a lot of drama. I assume because of his teenage hormones, it was difficult for him to date one person. Shawn seemed to have a habit of dating girls who made it known they were involved. I'm certain their efforts were to upset me and make me feel insecure. Based on my past, ignoring them became the most difficult thing I ever did. Hurting them physically would have given me great pleasure but I wanted something more. I was a part of something bigger than my relationship with Shawn. Being a part of pom-pom was always my excuse not to fight. The coaches made it clear that fighting was unacceptable and cause for suspension. While my provoking fights were over, it seemed the girl drama would never end. A few blocks from me, lived a young lady by the name of "D." We befriended each other for a short period of time but when it became clear that she and Shawn had sex with each other, our friendship ended. We often took the school bus together and in high school, when girls are no longer friends, every place they meet becomes a battle ground. I started sitting in the front of the bus to avoid hearing the name calling and the details of her and Shawn's moment. Needless to say it made me very upset and took everything I had to overlook "D" and her crew.

I tried to do something different with potential confrontations. If I ever felt threatened or feared that I would hit someone, I told my Dean, Mr. W. Mr. W was the most intimidating man I ever met. He reminded me of Lurch from the Adams Family and he never believed a word I said. I think it shocked Mr. W for me to come to him proactively. He saw my record and strongly assumed I would be a social misfit. I was surprised he had given me the benefit of the doubt and listened to my concerns. It was usually Mr. W's procedure to send a call slip, confront the person of concern and encourage them to behave or they would be suspended. "D" had a sidekick and for the sake of names, I'll call her "Big J". "Big J" didn't know me at all but she often sat at the back of the bus throwing paper at me and calling me names. She was much bigger than anyone I had ever battled, 6 feet tall and about 225 pounds. I knew that if she and I ever fought, it definitely wouldn't be a fair one.

Friday, October 13, 1995, I lost my first one on one fight. About a week before, I began to carry a knife to school just in case "Big J" tried to fight me. I spoke with Mr. W about my continuing to feel threatened and as he promised, "Big J" was suspended. The bus ride to school the next day seemed to be a relief until "Big J" got on. It never crossed my mind that she had nothing to lose so it only made sense that she would fight me anyway. I sat with my backpack in my lap as she walked up and pushed it on the ground. "You got me suspended and now I'm about to kick your ass." Dressed in my pom-pom uniform and thinking about the location of my knife, I chose not to back out of this fight. I stood up and before I could even position myself, she punched me. I fought back as hard as I could. As I subtly reached for my knife, it fell on the school bus floor. For the first time since that gun was pointed at me, I felt overpowered and helpless. "Big J" had the strongest hold to my hair as we tumbled from seat to seat. As usual, my nails were my weapon and I always used them as such. I believe for her to feel them in her face made her angrier. Her grip on my hair became tighter and tighter. At no shock to me, no one tried to break it up. The bus driver eventually stopped at the school and the students scattered back to their seats. I was very angry and disappointed when witnesses reported that Travis watched as this Amazon beat me up. While I had just lost a fight, all I could think about was my position on pom-pom being terminated. It didn't matter if people thought I was a punk. "Big J" was clearly bigger than me which meant, I didn't stand a chance. I was grateful that I didn't get in trouble for the knife and because I forewarned Mr. W, I was able to stay on pom-pom and attend school that day.

As we exited the bus, "Big J" and I were escorted to the dean's office. Walking down the hallway of red walls and grey lockers, I saw Jackie being escorted by police out of the Dean's office in handcuffs. "What did *you* do?" I asked her. "I whooped that bitch ass." She proudly responded. "Who?" I asked. Not able to stop and talk, she shouted from the end of the hall . . . "D!" I was confused as to how that happened so fast considering we just got off the bus. Similarly, Jackie never met "D" and had no clue what she looked like. I believe someone that knew the dynamics of me and Jackie's friendship made sure she knew that her best friend was just beaten up and the person behind it all was "D." I never wanted Jackie to get suspended on my account. She later told me that it really brought her to tears to hear about how "Big J" handled me. I can't remember who gave her the information but she said she asked this person to point "D" out and when they did, she asked no questions, walked up to her and began using all sorts of physical force. Still in disbelief about the timing and situation, I appreciated her for that and no matter who came into my life, Jackie would always come first.

Jackie supported the changes I attempted to make in my social life. She seemed proud that I turned in my baggie Cross Colours and boxing gloves for some pom-poms and skirt. She wanted to protect me from everyone, including Shawn. Shawn's issues were becoming more and more apparent. It seemed I had fallen in love with a manipulator. He avoided the traditional things teenagers did like school and work. I saw him struggle with being the man his parents wanted him to be and the man the streets wanted him to be. I wasn't sure if I would be with him forever or if this was just a phase and only time would tell how far he and I would go. I knew for certain I wanted him to finish school and experience things as I did. Unfortunately listening wasn't his strength and I became vulnerable to other people.

February 1996, Jackie was now driving and we decided to stop at Amoco in the town I use to live in. As I went in to pay for gas, I saw William. Although very different, he was more handsome than I imagined. He shaved his head bald and had a small feather earring hanging in his ear. He seemed happy to see me as I was with him. I told him about me living with my mother now and how much I've missed him. We exchanged numbers and began seeing each other as much as we could. When I saw William, my relationship with Shawn didn't cross my mind. I believe I grew tired of Shawn getting into trouble and missing out on life. He and I began to argue and fight about the many girls he slept with and I became nonchalant about who I wanted to see and what I wanted to do. Almost a week after William and I reconnected, he picked me up from the corner of my block. We went to his apartment and I remember losing all the inhibition and fear I had years before. The room was dark but lightened with a dim. I wore a blue denim dress that buttoned from top to bottom. I let him slowly take it off as he questioned my readiness. I assured him I was ready and had no reservations about giving myself to him. William and I finally did it. We continued to keep our relationship a secret for we had all things against us. I promised myself that I wasn't going anywhere and that as long as I was in his life, he would never be alone.

After I began seeing William, Shawn grew to be more of a gentleman. His behaviors often made me feel uncomfortable because he was either plotting or planning. I knew Shawn loved me for he often told me so and judging by his actions, I truly believed he knew something. However, he wanted me to believe he was making me more of a priority than it seemed. He started to buy me flowers, wait on me hand and foot and accepted my offer to be my date for a school dance. While I enjoyed Shawn's attempts to be a better boyfriend, there was always something he'd do to make me forget the good. While I no longer lived on 94th, my defenses were still up. I didn't let Shawn disrespect me and while I didn't fight in school, I had no problem fighting him. In our arguments, I made sure I got the last word. When he would push me, I would push him back and not once did I demonstrate fear or helplessness. Patsi never really got involved in our arguments. Depending on how she felt at the time, she might have asked Shawn to leave but nothing more. To avoid most of the drama with Patsi and Shawn, I found a part time job. It was only a matter of weeks before my 15th birthday so the school provided me with a work permit.

March 1996, I started working at Kentucky Fried Chicken in the mall. Like Pom-pom, working became my outlet. I had fun with my co-workers and enjoyed eating all the honey barbeque wings and corn muffins a girl could have. The money was useful in getting the things that Patsi refused to buy such as underwear and toiletries. I loved my job until the day I went and couldn't stand the smell. I stood there taking orders as I leaned over the counter. My supervisor often asked me to stand up but I couldn't. I felt ill on the inside and out. My body felt swollen, my breast felt tender to touch and I had a weird discharge coming from my vaginal area. I asked to go home early and my supervisor agreed. Once I got home, I told Patsi about my symptoms. Worried and concerned that I might be food poisoned, she suggested that we go to the emergency room. Worried like Patsi, Shawn asked to come along. We made it to the hospital and it was my turn to see the nurse. She took a urine sample and a blood sample. She asked me to sit on the table and the doctor would be in to see me. I remember feeling very nervous. I wore a burgundy sweat suit and watched as my Filas swung above the floor. She asked me to get undressed from the waist down but Patsi refused to let that happen. She argued that I was still a virgin therefore there was no need. I don't think Patsi really believed that because as she sat with me, I received the coldest blank stare. When she was worried about something or had things on her mind, her cheeks hung low and her lids never seemed to move. As the doctor walked in to see me, I knew he would tell me to let the food poison run its course. Unfortunately that didn't seem to be the information he wanted to share. Respectfully, he asked Patsi to leave the room. Not happy about the request, Patsi honored it. I heard an annoying squeaky sound as the door closed shut. The doctor leaned in towards me and asked, "Are you sexually active?" As I did with all the adults who asked that question my response was "Oh no, not me. I'm too scared for that." Laughing at my lie, the doctor looked at me and said, "That's funny because based on your urine and blood sample, you're about 4 weeks pregnant." Devastated and shocked, I was speechless. My heart immediately fell into my stomach and I could no longer breathe. Giving me no time to respond, he said he'd leave the room so I could get undressed from the waist down.

I felt my heart beating through my sweat shirt. The emergency room was now where I wanted to live. I felt safe there and there was no way I could tell Patsi I was pregnant. Checking to see if I was ready, the doctor knocked on the door. "Come in" I cried. He asked me to lie back and place my legs on the stirrups. I could hear his voice now . . . "Well Ms. Brown, judging from your discharge, it looks like you have Chlamydia. I'm going to give you an antibiotic shot that should clear this up in 5-7 days. I suggest you start using condoms." This immediately became too much news for me. I remember thinking, "I just started my health class. How could I be going through things I haven't learned about?" The doctor didn't seem very sympathetic to my situation. He explained my rights as a teenager and said that because I was over the age of 12 he didn't have to tell Patsi I was pregnant but had to tell her that I was sexually active. I suggested that he should tell her everything and so he did.

Chapter 10

Baby Momma

AFTER THE DOCTOR TOLD PATSI that I was sexually active and pregnant, it was as if someone had died. She looked at me with disappointment. It was as if she saw everything that went wrong in her life, suddenly going wrong in mine. I cried. I apologized. I even asked God for his forgiveness but I didn't feel like He or anyone else heard me. Shawn sat in the waiting room as Patsi walked out in disgust. She looked at him and said, "It's not food poisoning. She's pregnant *and* she has a venereal disease." Shawn looked at me with a smirk on his face as if things were going exactly as he planned it. "Wipe that stupid ass smile off your face." I said. He followed behind me chanting, "What? What?" The ride home was completely silent. Patsi didn't even look at me. Shawn followed us into the house and silently, Patsi went into her bedroom. I sat on the living room couch closest to the front door as Shawn sat in a chair at the dining room table. After almost 15 minutes of silence, Patsi walked out of her room, looked over the balcony and said, "So what are you going to do? Your ass can't stay here." With tears in my eyes, I looked up at her and said, "I don't know." I had so many questions and not a lot of answers. I was 14, pregnant with an STD and had no idea who else to hold responsible. The dates and times played over and over in my head. William and I used condoms and I knew nothing about who was in his life. Shawn and I never used condoms and he had a history of being with other girls.

The hardest decision was deciding whether or not to go through with this pregnancy and since I wasn't sure who the father was, I shared the information with William as well. William never denied that he could have been responsible but he did deny giving me an STD. I believed him for the timing of my symptoms didn't correlate with the time I was last with him. With sympathy and compassion, he said that the choice to keep the baby was mine and if the baby turned out to be his, he would be there. I didn't tell Shawn right away that there was someone else. However, I told Patsi and she immediately remembered William from when we first moved to the suburbs. She asked me to have William stop by the house so the two of them could formally meet. While I do recall him coming by and meeting Patsi, I don't remember how that conversation went.

I know that Patsi was clearly bothered by me and William's age difference. However, she seemed willing to turn the other cheek based on her guilt of dating older men *and* pending he'd buy her a pack of cigarettes every now and then. Nevertheless I was glad that the only people William needed to be a secret to, were the authorities, my dad and Shawn.

Shawn and I decided to tell his parents about the pregnancy over the phone. Shawn lived with his grandfather so it was easy to avoid his parents in case of a disaster. His mother seemed to take it very hard. I remember his brother sharing the news about his girlfriend's pregnancy almost a week earlier. As expected, many people were disappointed in our actions. It seemed that everyone who had faith that I would go far in academics, suddenly stopped believing in me. The verdict was that I'd be like Patsi and drop out. My aunt Cara began calling me and tried hard to convince me to have an abortion. Out of fear and confusion, I agreed to let her make me an appointment but when the time came, I didn't go. My aunt Phyllis vowed to never speak to me again. If there was anyone I never wanted to disappoint, it was definitely her. My dad blamed Patsi for everything that had gone wrong in my life and while I didn't want him to know about William, she sure told him. My dad's first reaction was to find Jackson, get together and hurt William for taking advantage of his little girl. I worked hard to convince both Jackson and my dad that I wanted William and that I was the one who seduced him. They wanted to meet him just as Patsi did and while William was willing to do that, I needed time to pass before that could happen. Truth of the matter still remained I didn't know who I was pregnant by. Shawn really wanted this child and while he and I didn't have the best relationship, I was willing to have it. Shawn denied sleeping with other girls and exposing me to Chlamydia. I didn't believe him and anyone that saw the girls he slept with, wouldn't have believed him either.

School was letting out soon and I tried very hard to keep the pregnancy to myself. I told Jackie about my pregnancy and coincidentally, her mother didn't believe she had food poisoning either. Jackie became serious with a guy she met in her neighborhood and I imagine that due to the amount of time they spent together, her mom wasn't convinced that she was fetus free. I will never forget the day Jackie called me going crazy about her mother making her urinate in a cup. Jackie's mom worked in a hospital so it seemed easy for her to test a urine sample. Jackie said she tried to tell her mother that there was nothing going on but she didn't believe her. About three days later, Jackie called me back to tell me that her pregnancy test was positive too. No one believed that Jackie and I did not have a pregnancy pact. I was convinced that because she and I were so close, what happened to one was bound to happen to the other. While logical to me, it made sense to no one else. Nevertheless, I was happy that I no longer had to face my fears alone.

Time passed and so did my birthday. There was no celebration for the pregnant girl. Patsi said she wanted me to understand that after children, parents no longer celebrated birthdays. While I didn't believe that to be true at all, I accepted the point she attempted to make. For a short time, it seemed all the fun suddenly stopped. According to Patsi, Connie's mom was cautious about letting her come over. It was supposedly said that I was a bad influence on Connie right before it came out that Connie was due with a child a month before I was. It was funny that as long as I was seen as this bright girl with good grades, my life would be perfect but as soon as that same bright girl gets pregnant, she immediately becomes the dumb bad influence. It seemed no one took into consideration that I still had strengths so I decided to go through with this pregnancy. I spent the summer going to doctor's appointments, preparing for this baby and battling Patsi. Her drinking increased and so did my stress levels. Unbeknownst to me, Shawn increased his involvement in criminal activity so he spent a lot of time in an out of juvenile detention. I didn't want this pregnancy to be the end of me and I damn sure didn't want to repeat the history of Patsi. I was told time and time again by Patsi that I wouldn't amount to anything. According to her, Shawn would leave me and so would William. If she were judge and jury, I would be forced to raise this baby on my own and my dreams would no longer be mine. The funny thing about that idea was that I didn't have any dreams. I never thought about having a man to take care of me. I never wanted to be a wife and I never thought about children. The only thing I thought of was being able to have my own so that I didn't have to be guided by hurt and pain like she was. I saw what loving my father did to her and I promised myself that love would never do that to me. Regardless of what my plans weren't I now had to develop one. I had no clue of who I wanted to be and how I was going to get there.

I struggled with whether or not Shawn was the best person for me. During his time in detention, I reconnected with old male friends and met new ones. I continued to see William and go on with my life as if this pregnancy was just a zit. Most of my male friendships I was forced to keep a secret and not because we were intimate but because Shawn would always try to intimidate them. My friend and confidant, Dedrick seemed to be the only male friend who wasn't intimidated by Shawn. Dedrick and I always had a special friendship. We met at Thunderbird. He was on the football team and one of the finest males I ever seen. Dedrick was light-skinned, often wore a low hair cut and had a body and smile out of this world. He was fit to be a model and had a very caring soul. I enjoyed being with Dedrick because we were clearly attracted to one another but our friendship was more of an asset. He didn't like the way Shawn was treating me and would sometimes be my safe haven when I needed to get away. I thought it was amazing how many male friends were willing to be there for me like Dedrick was but sometimes it just wasn't safe.

My fourth month into my pregnancy, I went to visit some old friends from my old town. It was refreshing to get away from the house and laugh for no reason at all. I hung out with them most of that night and because it was getting late one of the guys in the group decided to take me home. He pulls up to the house and I was pleased that Shawn appeared to be nowhere in sight. It was dark outside so my friend didn't pull off until I made it to the door. As he made it to the corner, I heard glass shattering. I saw Shawn along with his friend running towards the house from the direction of the sound. He was laughing and when he made it to me, he smacked me. We began to fight and I don't think his friend expected me to fight back as hard as I did. Shocked and concerned about the baby, he broke it up. Shawn complained that I disrespected him by having some guy drop me off. I often ignored his feelings because he clearly no longer cared about mine.

Later that week and in a heated argument, I decided to tell Shawn about William. I know he was hurt for he turned his back and started chanting, "The baby ain't mine! The baby ain't mine!" I don't know if he took me seriously for he went on dealing with me as if I said nothing. I know those that cared about me really wanted me to leave Shawn. While many people didn't like my relationship, they respected it. I imagine that many of my friends thought that if they pushed me to leave, it would only provoke resentment. I stayed with him because I cared about him. I thought I loved him and hoped he would change.

Between the physical battles with Shawn and the verbal battles with Patsi, it seemed I could never get a break. I was never quiet and timid in my reactions but continuously having to fight my mother and my boyfriend, was exhausting. My friends became everything to me. While Jackie was constant, Thunderbird introduced me to a very supportive group of ladies. We had a lot in common and being with them was the only time I could behave like my life was healthy. Renay, Leslie, Sky and Lynn were my rocks. I met Renay and Leslie through Pom-pom. Renay was short in height; light skinned and had the pretties eyes and soul. She brought a lot of joy in my life with her kind heart and mild temperament. I thought it was funny how Renay always tried to preach to me about morals. She almost reminded me of Leslie. Leslie was like a big sister to me. She was two years older than me and had impeccable style. Leslie often lectured me about the importance of self-respect and God. What I loved most about her was her ability to see my hurt and stick by me despite it all. Sky and I became friends through Renay. Like me and Jackie, Sky and I didn't take too kind to each other initially but as Renay did with everyone, she brought us together. I saw Sky as my "ride or die" buddy. She often had my back and I had hers. We spent a lot of time hanging out or shall I say, riding down 79th & Stoney. I don't think I laughed as hard with anyone as much as I laughed with

Sky. I could be myself, attitude and all and there wasn't anything, she ever tried to change about me. When I wasn't hanging out with Sky, Lynn and I were probably getting into trouble. Not that any of the other girls didn't, Lynn and I could always relate when it came to the males. I didn't feel judged when it came to my relationship with William or desires to be with others. Lynn was probably one of two friends that actually had sex as much as I did and no one knew about it. She had the prettiest caramel skin, the highest cheek bones and the prettiest smile. While she didn't always see it, she was very beautiful. I often grew tired of telling Lynn that at a size 7, she wasn't overweight as I'm sure she grew tired of telling me that William was too old for me.

Another summer was ending and school was about to start. This was the first time anyone would see me pregnant. While students heard the rumors, no one knew for sure and those that did were in disbelief. I will never forget going to registration. I wore a blue and white baby doll dress. The mumps in my stomach were very apparent and the first to notice was Natasha. "Oh my God, you really are pregnant." She said it with such joy and I smiled with such embarrassment. I knew that I couldn't hide my stomach and I actually didn't want to. I know others judged and criticized but that only made me stronger. Shawn and I didn't seem to be making progress as a couple. It seemed to be our norm to argue, makeup, fight, argue, makeup and fight again. Patsi's overwhelming changes in personality went from making my favorite red beans and rice to calling me bitches and whores, wishing I'd never been born. My doctor told me that all the stress could have harmful effects on my pregnancy and I was determined not to let that happen. Coming to school every day pretending to be ok was getting old. I believed I reached a breaking point and had to tell someone what I was going through.

Wednesday, October 9, 1996, I requested to see Mrs. C. Mrs. C was my counselor and now my sounding board. I no longer cared about what others knew about my household. I needed an outlet and she was there to listen. I cried and cried as I told Mrs. C. about the verbal abuse from my mother, the physical and emotional trauma from Shawn and my fears with having a baby. She was very sympathetic to my situation and it seemed she wanted to cry with me. She suggested that I get involved in a teen parenting group and provided me with contact information for Janet Roberson. Mrs. C. also suggested that I change my homeroom in an effort to gain support and have access to all the resources available to teen moms. Unbeknownst to her, Mrs. C. changed my life forever.

Chapter 11

Break
Away

I WAS NOW 8 MONTHS pregnant and soon to be the mother of a son. Patsi had given me a baby shower and it turned out to be very nice. All of my friends and family attended and for the first time since becoming pregnant, I felt ready. There was nothing more I could do about the past. I challenged myself to let go of the poor choices I made and although very hard, I managed. When Patsi did nice things for me, it almost felt surreal. I often asked myself, "Why can't she be like this all of the time?" I accepted it anytime she wanted to help because I knew the alcohol often magnified her problems. Still our issues were far from over and after the baby was born, things would only get worse.

Ameer was born December 30, 1996 at 11:18pm. He was 7 pounds, 3 ounces and 19 ½ inches long. I was in labor 11 hours with no medicine and one stitch. I remember the day he was born like it was yesterday. December 29th, Shawn and I were actually getting along. Patsi often allowed him to spend the night as long as he stayed out of my room. As Patsi slept upstairs, I snuck down in the basement to "watch television" with him. The next morning I got up in severe pain. I called my doctor and she told me to wait an hour before going to the hospital. The hour passed and the pain became more intense. Patsi took me to the hospital and I learned that I dilated 4 centimeters. They decided to admit me and 9 hours later I only dilated 1 centimeter more. Patsi promised she'd return with Shawn so that he didn't miss the birth of his son. I thought about calling William but I knew it would bring more drama than I was ready for. The doctor decided to break my water and I must admit that was the worst thing a doctor could ever do to a patient.

The contractions were coming faster and faster and still I declined medication. Shawn showed up with candy, flowers, a teddy bear and a balloon. He said he caught a ride because Patsi didn't want to bring him. I don't know what happened to Patsi between the time she dropped me off at the hospital and the time I started to push. She showed up drunk and cursing at the nurse demanding that Shawn leave the room. We thought she would calm down but she didn't. I pushed for almost an hour and one could tell that the doctor was annoyed by Patsi's behavior. It was time to cut the umbilical cord and as most doctors did, she handed the scissors to Shawn. It was at that moment, Patsi lost it! Addressed to the doctor, Patsi shouted, "How dare you let him cut the umbilical cord? That's my muthafuckin' daughter and she came out of my pussy. He has no right to even be here." The doctor remained calm and tried to reason with Patsi by explaining that Shawn was the father and he had every right to be there and if she couldn't handle it then maybe *she* should leave. Patsi stormed out of the room without taking a look at Ameer. I was embarrassed and as usual, Shawn had that damn smirk on his face.

I was relieved to have that baby out of me. I heard breast milk was the best milk and since I finally got some breasts, I thought nursing would be a good idea. Ameer was an awesome baby and considering everything I experienced during my pregnancy, he seemed very happy. The next day Shawn's family came to visit and while they still weren't very fond of me, they embraced and accepted Ameer as one of their own. It seemed Shawn's mom tried to warm up to me. She attended the baby shower and she now said more than a sentence. I imagine she didn't like Ameer's name because she kept calling him "whats-his-face." She examined Ameer from top to bottom, taking off all of his clothes, checking his fingers and toes. It caught her attention that Ameer had a distinctive physical trait, one that reportedly ran in the family. It was at that moment, I believed she was convinced that Ameer belonged in her family. Later that day, Patsi showed up at the hospital. She was sober and claimed she couldn't remember anything that happened the night before. She walked in bragging about this handsome baby in the nursery and how he had on purple and I just had to see him. I thought it was amazing how Patsi could almost ruin a person's life and then go on like nothing ever happened. I entertained the thought and I asked the nurse to bring Ameer to me for a feeding. I also wanted Patsi to see him regardless of her inappropriate behaviors. She was his grandmother whether I liked it or not and deserved to be around him just as Shawn's mother had.

The nurse strolls in the room with the baby in purple. Patsi shouted, "Oh my God, that's *my* grandbaby?" Patsi had the biggest smile on her face and I don't think I ever seen her so happy. I could tell that holding Ameer did something to her. It was as if she was holding Darren again. She fell in love and said she would be the best grandmother she could. It made me happy to see her happy but I didn't trust that she would stop drinking. I learned to pick and choose my battles with Patsi so when I wanted to say something that could potentially start an argument, I didn't. After a day or so in the hospital, I was allowed to go home. Grandma Reese, Connie's mom, Lori and the rest of the gang all came to see Ameer. He was now the cutest baby I had ever seen (not that I had seen many). He had the chubbiest cheeks, the most perfect round head, the nicest hair and rolls in every joint on his body as if they were strictly made for fat. I was glad that I had him and I was proud that I hadn't given up. The turn-around for Patsi's mood swing was half a day. The day I came home, she still didn't want Shawn spending time with his son. He came to visit and as he and Lori stood in my room, Patsi yelled for him to get out of her house. Shawn didn't have too many confrontations with Patsi. He often listened when she spoke. I felt bad that she treated him that way. I believe he understood that she wasn't "all there." He left and came back later. There was no doubt in my mind that Shawn wanted to be a father to Ameer.

A day or two passed since I returned from the hospital. I finally decided to call William. He seemed hurt that I didn't call him from the hospital but understood why. While many people were convinced that Shawn was the father, William wanted to see Ameer for himself. William had a theory that his mother always knew her grandchildren and could tell just by looking if a child belonged in her family or not. I knew deep down inside, I wanted this little boy to be William's. We took him to meet William's mother and she looked at him and said, "I don't know William." As time went on, Ameer didn't share any features of Williams and there was still the distinct physical trait Ameer shared with Shawn and his dad. William and I agreed that Ameer was *not* his and we would go on with our lives as we had.

Being a new mom was not as difficult as I thought it would be. My greatest challenge was finding childcare for when I returned to school. Patsi agreed to keep Ameer for a small fee and with little to no options, I agreed. I still worked at KFC up until Ameer was born and I was scheduled to go back to work when my maternity leave ended. Shawn started a job sometime before Ameer was born. It was a seasonal job for the holidays and somehow he managed to keep it. Since Shawn was no longer in school, Patsi had a bright idea that while I pay her, she would ask Shawn to be with his son. I was a little confused with that arrangement based on our agreement but I was still in no condition to argue with Patsi.

Monday, February 3, 1997, I was expected to return to school. Patsi said she spoke with Shawn and he agreed to be at our house before I got on the school bus. As I got dressed, Patsi decided to go to the store. She said she needed to get her a pack of cigarettes. While the store was not that far away, she managed to make it back very quickly. She walked into the house and asked me had I heard from Shawn. Tying up my shoe strings, I looked up at her and said, "Nope." With a sneaky tone in her voice she said, "Go look in the garage. I want to show you something." Curious about what she wanted me to see, I led the way to the back door. As I made it to the garage, I noticed a bronze colored vehicle pulled in halfway. The car looked very familiar. I often saw it parked in Shawn's driveway. With certainty, I turned to Patsi and said, "That's Shawn's grandfather's car. Shawn's probably in their sleep. Is this all you wanted to me to see?" Shaking her head at me, she replies, "Silly girl, look a little closer." I stepped in a little further to get a better view. It was pretty cold outside so the windows were a little frosty. The closer I got, I saw what appeared to be Shawn's coat in the passenger seat. Then I also saw a woman's body moving up and down. It later made sense that the coat was covering her backside. I walked up to the passenger side window and saw Shawn with is head tilted back not even recognizing that I'm standing there. It is evident that he and this woman are having sex in *her* car which is parked in *my* garage.

I imagine by this time I was just tired. Patsi witnessed as I lost my breath and became speechless. She instructed with firm demand, "Pick up that brick and throw it through the window." I couldn't move and I was in shock that he still didn't notice me standing there. Was it that good that he no longer became aware of his surroundings? I had seen enough and Patsi grew tired of me standing there so she picked up the brick and threw it at the window. The woman jumped off Shawn as he hurried to pull up his pants. I began to cry and bang on the hood of the car as she pulled out of my garage. Patsi seemed ready to fight and at the same time began chanting, "I told you what would happened after you had that baby, didn't I?" With tears flooding my face, I grabbed my coat and book bag and headed to school. As I walked to the bus stop, Shawn pulls up on the side of me. "What's wrong?" he asked. "Why are you crying?" It was at that moment, I could have choked him but all I could think about was Ameer. Earlier, when I ran into the house to get my coat and book bag, Ameer seemed to have felt my pain. As soon as he heard my cry, he began to scream like someone pinched him in his sleep. I ignored Shawn's homicidal provoking question and continued to walk. With no shame or care, he still had the woman in the car with him. I continued to ignore him. As far as I was concerned, he and I were over. My only concerns from this point on were completing school and caring for my son.

Chapter 12

Emancipation

S HAWN TRIED FOR DAYS AND days to talk to me. I was done with him and there was nothing he could say or do to change that. We often got into scuffles as he waited for me at my bus stop. I didn't care that he was Ameer's father. I wanted him out of my life. When things were sometimes overwhelming, I went back to God. I know I should've always gone to Him but in the mind of a "half-saved" teenager, there was this misperception that one only calls on God when they're hurting. For nights, I would close my bedroom door, get on my knees and pray that God take Shawn out of my life. I didn't want him to die. I just wanted peace. When I thought God didn't hear me, I wrote a letter and stuck it in the Bible. It didn't matter which chapter or verse because from what I heard, it was all God's word.

I'm not quite sure what happened but for a while, I didn't hear from Shawn. He didn't call. He didn't come by the house and that was alright with me. I didn't inquire with his friends or family and they never inquired about me. Patsi was bonding very well with Ameer. He had become her baby and she seemed proud to be a grandmother. She baby sat most days and took him to spend time on 94th with Grandma Reese and the rest of the family. I remember Patsi dressing him up in the cutest print sleepers. She would throw on his hooded blue and red jacket and place sunglasses on his face. Everyone loved Ameer. This was the first time since Hazel had there been a baby in the family. Hazel would be turning 5 soon and with her living in California, the family missed having a young one around. There were other babies in the family but we didn't get to see them unless it was a holiday or a random visit. My cousin Lori was pregnant with her second child and many of us couldn't wait because she waited almost nine years to have him. Connie had her son and he was born a month before Ameer was (guess I wasn't the bad influence after all). While I tried to keep up with Connie and spend time, it wasn't happening. Shawn's brother also had a son who was born 6 months before Ameer. I admired that Shawn's family made strong efforts to make sure the two boys knew they were family.

1997 was a good year for me. Since having to give up Pom-pom, I had to do other things to keep myself busy. I changed jobs from KFS to Footlocker. I became active in teen parenting groups and programs. I finally met Janet Roberson, the woman Mrs. C. referred me to. She was the facilitator of a teen parenting project. I will never forget the day she visited the teen parent's homeroom. It was fall school year of 1997. She pitched the program to us and told us all these great things about going to college and the importance of raising our babies in a healthy environment. It wasn't until then I thought about even going to another school after high school. Only a small percentage of my family completed high school (3 people) so I was certain, no one could fathom me going to college. I knew my grades were strong and I didn't worry about whether or not a school would accept me. When I heard it had to be paid for, I was immediately discouraged. After Mrs. Roberson's pitch, I spoke with her and gave her bits and pieces of my story. She suggested that I get Ameer in the school district's daycare so that I can spend more time with her and her group. Mrs. Roberson knew about the other group I participated in and she suggested that I complete it. While the focus of the two groups was different, they were equally helpful. The other group was facilitated by Mrs. Thompson. Mrs. Thompson was very compassionate about our group. The group was facilitated at a church in my town. If I recall, we often met twice a week. There was a shuttle bus that provided transportation from school to home. This group was designed to prevent a second pregnancy before completing high school. While it didn't give me the tools to go to college, it focused on relationship issues, birth control, STD's and different forms of abuse. Unfortunately, I had been affected by all of that and for very different reasons both groups were well needed in my life.

I often thought about how I was going to manage everything in my life. I was already a part of two groups. I was working 20 hours a week and still had to finish school. I hadn't spent much time with Ameer and I wasn't expected to graduate until 1999. I couldn't imagine doing this routine and putting up with Shawn and Patsi for another two years. Something had to change and because I wasn't sure about what that *something* was, I did what I made a habit of doing, talking to Mrs. C. I put in a request to see her and about half way through the day, I got a call slip. I told her about my desires to get away from my family as fast as I could. Now that I had this idea of going to college I wanted to go that day. One would think the support groups were selling me dreams but I realized they weren't *selling* me anything and what happened in my future was all up to me. I believe she understood what message I was trying to convey to her but I didn't believe she could do anything about it. "Let me take a look at your grades and GPA," she said. She faced her screen, clicked on her mouse and started writing on a notepad. I had no idea what she was doing but when she was done, she turned to me and said, "If you can take a 0 period PE class and two English courses by the end of the school year, I can graduate you with the class of 1998." I became teary eyed for she fast forwarded my life. Without hesitation, I agreed to change my academic plans.

Things seemed to be coming along great. Ameer started going to the daycare at Wildcat High School and while Patsi was no longer happy with that, I had to do what was best for us. My schedule was hectic. Every day for the next 6 months, I woke up at 4 am, to make the school bus by 5:30, get to my 0 period by 6:30, finish my school day, get on a shuttle and go to my first group, pick up Ameer, get on another shuttle bus and go to my second group, get home, do homework and go to bed. The groups weren't in session every day so I also made time for work. Patsi still was able to spend time with Ameer on the weekends and some week nights. She often kept him while I worked and I don't think it bothered her because she convinced herself that Ameer was her son. When I had days off, she encouraged me to hang out and spend time with my friends. I took her up on her offers especially since Jackie and I reconnected with Carly.

Carly transferred to Thunderbird in 1997 and it was good to be around her again. We all clearly changed and weren't like we use to be but nevertheless, the love was still the same. Jackie and Carly played auntie to Ameer as I played Godmom to Jackie's daughter. I must say that I was the worst God mom a child could ever have and

I know it was because I was so self-consumed. As to be expected, Jackie was not happy that I didn't make her Ameer's Godmother. I thought it would be best if I gave the role to someone who was in *his* family, especially since my dear friend Dedrick accepted the offer to be Ameer's Godfather. During my pregnancy, I grew close to Shawn's cousin, Effy. Effy seemed to take a genuine interest in me and my pregnancy. Since it seemed she and I shared the same desires in life, I thought it would be best to make her Ameer's Godmother. In hindsight that was one of the worst decisions I ever made. Effy graduated Thunderbird class of 1997 and shortly after that, I stopped hearing from her. She caught Patsi in one of her drunken moments and needless to say, Patsi wasn't very nice to her. While many of my friends knew Patsi was an alcoholic, they didn't shun *me* because of it. Many of them knew that I was a victim too. I suppose Effy didn't see it that way.

In the midst of learning who my real friends were, I still hung out with Renay, Sky and Lynn. Leslie left to attend college in Carbondale so we didn't get to speak that often. I met a new friend through the teen parenting program by the name of Porsha. She was new to the district and while many people didn't know her, a lot of them didn't like her. On many levels I could relate due to my experience at Jr. High2. I imagine it was because she was gorgeous, had height, a lovely figure and hair that flowed like Pocahontas. In my peers' defense, Porsha *did* carry herself with distance and wasn't as open to meeting others as I was. By spending time with her in the group, I was able to get to know Porsha therefore understood her behaviors better than the average classmate. While l loved my friends who appeared to have drama free lives, I had a desire to connect with girls I thought were more like me. With that being said, Porsha and I became close. Jackie didn't like her too much and neither did Sky. I didn't force them to hang out together and I never felt compelled to explain to them why I cared so much about her. To do that meant telling someone else's story and I had enough drama of my own.

I started dating again and opened myself up to what I thought was a world of quality. I began seeing guys who were playing football, going to college on scholarships, spending money on me and being gentlemen. Many of them made my relationship with Shawn look so juvenile. Somehow I reconnected with Luke and we picked up right where we left off. It seemed he was no longer mad at me for almost ruining his life. We hung out and talked pretty often. William became the constant secret in my life but I started to see that dealing with him wasn't the healthiest thing for me either. By now I had learned that men showed emotion by marking territory and taking control. William had a weird way of showing he cared about me it just didn't involve talking to me like he had some sense. He was often jealous of other males but clearly did what he wanted to do. I used it to my advantage that I wasn't 'legal' and according to our contract, our relationship didn't exist.

Months went by and I still hadn't heard from Shawn. I continued to stay on track with my academic plans but as Mrs. Roberson helped me prepare for college, I hit a couple of road blocks. Mrs. Roberson spent a lot of her time helping me complete the FASFA and numerous college applications. We searched high and low for universities that were family friendly. Our greatest challenge was getting me the financial assistance I needed without Patsi's help. When Patsi got drunk, she sometimes threw me and Ameer out of the house leaving me to find some place to sleep overnight. When that happened by definition, I became homeless. In the state of Illinois, there were only so many categories a teenager could fit under to become emancipated as a minor. Mrs. Roberson and my dad had this bright idea that with a son and occasional homelessness, I fit one of the categories. We filed a motion with the courts to release me from the minor status. I believe one or more of my parents had to support the idea that I was taking care of myself in order for this to work. My dad was definitely a supporter because my "no longer being a minor" meant, he no longer had to pay child support. I will never forget the day my dad and I went to court. I was a witness to the fact that I was a parent with adult responsibilities and he was a witness to the number of times Patsi put me out. At no surprise to us, the judge granted the motion and at 16, I was legally an adult.

Chapter 13
Moving On

WITH THINGS GOING SO SMOOTHLY, I started to believe God was answering my prayers. I was making decent money at Footlocker and had the best co-workers in the world. We often spent a lot of time laughing, checking out the newest Jordans before they were released and being bullied by the managers when it came time to get their lunch. I met a lot of celebrities with that job; Flava Flav, R. Kelly and Do or Die. I also met a lot of men with that job and for the first time I no longer believed it mattered that I had brown skin. The men who seemed untouchable were starting to like me too. Regardless of how many men fell for me, it seemed William became priority. While many people couldn't prove that William and I had a relationship, they assumed there was something going on. William never volunteered information about his love life. Somehow the information would just fall into my lap.

While I stood in town waiting for the bus to work, I ran into an old friend from church. For the same of names, I will call him Ace. Ace was one that knew me from choir and his working in the audio room with Phyllis. He also thought he knew about me and William and not knowing that he really didn't, I would soon learn the downfall of talking too much. He asked how I was doing and said he heard that I had a baby. I confirmed that I was doing well and that my son would be turning one soon. He asked about William and since he appeared to know that William was in my life, I responded, "He's doing well. I was just with him." Ace then asked, "Did you know that William is getting married? I work with him and his fiancé and she's due to have a baby any day now." In total shock, my heart was suddenly broken. I wasn't sure whether or not to believe him because I hadn't seen Ace in years. I couldn't help but wonder how he benefited from sharing such information? I sucked back the tears and took my bus ride to work. Once I got to Footlocker, I was informed that I received several calls from William. He called again and this time I answered, "Thank you for calling World Footlocker, this is Nya." "Nya, what did Ace tell you?" He asked. "He told me that you were getting married. Is that true?" William had a way of avoiding questions but always asking them and expecting to get answers. "That's neither here nor there. I need you to do me a favor." I was not in the mood to do any favors for him but I definitely wanted to hear what he wanted. He told me that a woman was about to call me and to tell her that he and I stopped seeing each other a while ago. He told me the woman's name and made me promise to stick to the story he gave. As any woman scorned would, I promised to stick to the story and when she called, I told her what *I* wanted her to know.

Later that evening, William stopped by my house appearing to be in distress. He seemed sad about me telling his fiancé what I believed to be the truth about us. Lifting his pinky finger to show me the ring he gave her, he told me she had broken off the engagement. I imagine he wanted my sympathy and while I had never seen him so sad, I couldn't help but think, "Fuck you and what about me?" By this time William had been in my life 4 years. I expected him to care for me. I will never forget his words, "B, l love you. I really do but I *love, love* her." It was at that moment that I realized I had to let him go. I knew that because of my age, there would always be someone else. I wanted him to *love, love* me but if there was one thing I knew how to do by now, it was accept my losses.

Now that William was gone and Shawn remained nowhere to be found, I had time to focus on me. I submitted several college applications and crossed my fingers that some place would say "Yes." My relationship with Patsi was as to be expected considering she no longer received child support, food stamps or a medical card in my name. I believe she wanted to get back at me for she let the devil back into my life. The time was now March 1998. I received a suspicious phone call from a detective. He said that Shawn had been in police custody for quite some time and they were releasing him on house arrest. The detective then stated that Shawn listed our address as a possible place of residence. I told the detective that Shawn living with us wouldn't be a good idea but once he figured out I wasn't the owner of the residence, how I felt didn't seem to make a difference. Patsi took the phone from me and began speaking to the detective. I'm in the background, cueing her to say, "No!" Unfortunately, she said "Yes" and my life instantly became hell all over again.

Patsi tried to convince me that letting Shawn stay with us was the best thing to do. She said he needed to get to know his son and while I agreed Ameer should know his father, I didn't agree with us living together. I worried about my life, my new friends, my freedom and most of all, my plan to leave. It seemed that God didn't answer my prayer at all and boy was I mad at Him. I went on with my life as best I could. Ameer continued to go to the daycare and I continued to embrace my parenting group and all the assets I had at the time. Patsi clearly didn't care about how I felt. I can remember her and Shawn sitting at the dining room table discussing how stuck up and arrogant I'd become. I often ignored them. I was convinced that Patsi was jealous of me. I continued to make plans and didn't include her in any of them. I never told her I was going to college or that I even wanted to go. I believed I was literally sleeping with my enemies and my home became a battlefield.

A couple of months passed and it was time to prepare for prom. The extra classes, the job and being a parent was starting to wear on me. Shawn did exactly what I thought he would and intimidated all the male friends I had. Dedrick was off studying at a college up north so it seemed he dodged all the drama. Outside of him, I don't think there was one person sane enough to ask me to prom. There was one guy in school that actually seemed serious about taking me. I often didn't take him seriously because he was the class flirt so chances were he asked everybody. For the sake of names, I'll call him Leon. Leon was funny and the only person who made me laugh without trying. Leon was handsome. He was always well groomed. Like Dedrick, he played football as well. He was very popular and had a good heart. I enjoyed being around him and while I didn't believe we would actually go to prom together, I hoped we would. We attempted to shop for accessories and he often joked about seeing me in lingerie on prom night. I wasn't convinced at all that Leon was joking because if I was in agreement, he would've allowed it. Nevertheless I didn't entertain the idea and I reassured him that we were just friends and he wasn't getting any. I'm not certain that was our reason for never making it to prom but I later got a call from him stating that his parents wanted him to take a young lady from his church. Part of me felt like Leon was convinced not to take me because of Shawn. While I was hurt by not having a date, I still planned to go.

I struggled financially with paying for prom and almost didn't make it. I asked Patsi for money to buy a prom dress and her response was, "You mean to tell me that you're out here fuckin' and have no money for a prom dress? That doesn't make any sense to me." I often lost the battle trying to explain to Patsi that I wasn't a prostitute. I gave up asking her for help and I went back to Mrs. C. April 6, 1998, Mrs. C. sent me a call slip to come and see her. I told her about my problems with prom and she offered to help. She spoke with some other staff members who offered to pitch in and buy my dress, get my ticket and accessories. I was forever grateful to those that helped and if it weren't for them, I would have never made it to prom. Prom wasn't scheduled until May so I had a little time to get the things I did not have. I spent long hours with the girls in the group after school and sometimes I didn't make it home until close to 7pm. Wednesday, May 13, 1998, I came home tired and needing to study. Finals were around the corner and I hadn't even thought about graduation. Shawn sat on the porch as Ameer and I got off the shuttle. I asked him to watch Ameer as I studied and took a shower. He agreed so I left him out on the porch. Later that evening when Ameer came back into the house, he wreaked of this weird smell. I gave him a bath and we went to bed as usual. Thursday, May 14, 1998 as I walked down the hallway at school, I was stopped by a fellow classmate and neighbor who seemed desperately eager to tell me something. She told me that she tried to see me the night before but Shawn wouldn't let her come in the house. When I asked her what was on her mind, she told me that while Shawn was on the porch, he and his friends were smoking marijuana. I wasn't shocked for this is something Shaws always did but then she told me that he and his friends took turns blowing the smoke in Ameer's mouth. Suddenly the weird smell Ameer had made sense to me and I was now ready to fight. I ran past her to the social worker's office, begging him to use the phone. He allowed me to call home and Patsi answered. "Hello," she said. "Ma, let me speak to Shawn," I demanded. "Why do you sound upset? Calm down," she said. I told her what I had just been informed and she was in disbelief. She put me on hold and asked Shawn if what I said were true. He yelled from the background, "I didn't blow it in his mouth. I blew it in his face so tell that bitch to get her facts straight." Patsi returned to the phone and said, "He said he blew it in his face. A little smoke won't hurt nobody. I smoked when I was pregnant with you." It was at that moment, I wanted to kill her too. I called off work that evening because I wanted to catch the bus home and kick his ass. I jumped off the school bus, ran into the house and without introduction, smacked Shawn in his face. We began fighting all over the living room. Patsi broke up the fight and Shawn decided that he had enough. I told him to leave and that I wanted him out of my mother's house. I told him that I no longer cared about what happened to him as long as he was away from me. I imagine hearing those words come from me hurt his feelings. He looked at me, went into the kitchen, grabbed a knife, cut off his ankle monitor, sat the knife down, balled up his fist, took one last punch at me and ran out of the door. As I sat there holding my face, Patsi looked down from the balcony and said, "He should've whooped your ass. I would've punched you too."

Whether I was right or wrong, I just wanted this nightmare to be over. A couple of days later I received a phone call from the same detective. He asked me where Shawn was. I told him about what happened and that I had no idea where he'd gone. He told me that Shawn was with a young lady and that the two of them was wanted for murder and carjacking. He began to preach to me about the consequences of interfering with a police investigation. He said that if I knew anything and wasn't sharing, I would be in trouble. I assured the officer that I wasn't withholding any information and in fact wanted to get my 'lick' back from Shawn's punch. The detective stated that if he didn't find Shawn within 24 hours, he was going to the media. When I hung up the phone, I definitely feared for my safety. I knew Shawn was mad at me and I had no idea who this young lady was or what she was capable of. Patsi and I didn't have much to say to each other but she clearly had compassion for Shawn and wanted him to be alright.

As the detective promised, Shawn's story was aired on the news. I watched in disappointment and fear as they talked about a man being killed in another state and another shot locally. I knew he had a bad side to him but I thought, would he really kill someone? Who was I kidding? This was the same boy who often told me his dream was to make the news. As if my life at home wasn't enough, I had to face the interrogation of my peers the next day. As I walked down the hall at school, there was question after question about how and why did I fall for a guy like that. Those that knew Shawn and knew me seemed more sympathetic. Renay, Lynn, Sky, Porsha, Jackie, Carly all came together to support me and make sure that *I* was alright. They often hugged me, sat with me during lunch and offered to spend as much time with me as possible. According to the media, Shawn was still on the run and I had to figure out how to stay safe.

Saturday, May 16, 1998. I couldn't worry about Shawn and I needed to get ready for prom. Our lights were shut off and Patsi suggested that I get dressed on 94th. I found a date almost a week before this so I was pleased that I didn't have to go alone. I opted to get dressed with no lights so Patsi said she'd stick around for pictures and to meet my date. I forced myself to be happy on this day. I needed to be happy on this day. I worked too hard to get here and couldn't wait for my date to pick me up. My friends stopped by along with a few family members to see me off. I wore a blue beaded dress that crossed in the back and my date looked just like Puff Daddy. He was so handsome. We agreed to go as friends and nothing more. He already had a girlfriend and because she couldn't attend, I was more than happy to take her place as his date. After seeing me off, Patsi left along with Ameer to 94th. We made a few stops before heading to prom and I called Grandma Reese to check on Ameer. She told me that she was worried because Shawn stopped by with a young lady. She told me that they were both dressed in black and wanted to take Ameer with them. Grandma Reese said she firmly told them "No" but most importantly wanted me to be careful.

Grandma Reese added that the young lady seemed very interested to know what I looked like and that I should stay out as late as I could. To hear my grandmother tell me all of this brought extreme fear to my heart. While Shawn and I fought, I never believed he would try to take my life. However, I did believe that if given the opportunity, the young lady might have.

I had too much to plan for and I knew that life wasn't over for me just yet. I went to prom and had a great time. I laughed and danced with my friends and thought positive thoughts as graduation was less than a month away. May 17, 1998, I saw on the news that Shawn and the young lady was taken into custody by the police. While this was a happy moment for me, I deeply ached for Ameer. While I knew my son would need his father I often asked myself if having someone like that around would be helpful to him. I hated that our relationship became so toxic but people say things happen for a reason. I guess God really did answer my prayers just not in the way I thought He would.

Saturday, June 6, 1998, I graduated from high school. Outside of Shawn going to prison, this was the happiest day of my life. I later received my acceptance letter to a university down state with full financial aid and a small scholarship. They offered me a two bedroom apartment on campus along with on-campus daycare. Well needed and appreciated, I became the recipient of my own food stamps and medical card. While I didn't have transportation, I wasn't a stranger to the bus or train. I wasn't afraid to leave because I knew God would protect me. I thought to myself, "If I could function in this much chaos, imagine how powerful I would be in peace." Just as I designed it, Patsi had little to no involvement in my going to college. I told her very little about what was happening. I didn't believe she would be supportive or even understand the changes I was about to make. However, I was worried about Brittany. As much as we didn't get along, she wasn't as strong as I seemed to be and there was no way she could stand up to Patsi. I trusted Grandma Reese would care for Brittany if there was ever a need. I spent the summer tying up loose ends with work, and packing up all I owned. Surprisingly, Patsi gave me a graduation party making it harder to leave. I put a hault to potential romantic loves that promised to be there for me if I ever needed them.

The worst part about moving on was that I had to say goodbye to my friends. They were my sounding boards and the people I believe God put on this earth for comfort. My girls were my frame of reference for what genuine love and loyalty really looked like. Unfortunately, I had to go forward without them. The most honest thing my father ever told me was that I couldn't slow down so that others could catch up. I promised myself that I would always stand by that phrase; With that being said, I packed my bags, grabbed my baby and I left.

Acknowledgements

T O MY FAMILY . . . WE DIDN'T have much but we had each other and while we didn't always get along, it was your guidance that showed me the importance of loyalty.

To my mother, I know you did the best you could and I love you for making me strong.

To my girls, words cannot express how much your friendships mean to me. Without each of you (whether you're still a part of my life or not), I would be lost.

To counselors and social workers . . . where would the world be without you? Keep making the difference!

To my readers, I hope sharing my story gave you inspiration as well as motivation to do something you never thought you could do. Walking away from what's familiar to us can sometimes be very challenging. Many of us get caught up in our fears and fall victim to those that say we can't or won't be successful. Remember, a person's past doesn't have to be their future and with positive people, a plan and faith, one can do anything their heart desires.

Thank You

www.ingramcontent.com/pod-product-compliance
Lightning Source LLC
Chambersburg PA
CBHW020254290526
45784CB00003B/1248